Stochastic Interest Rates

This volume in the *Mastering Mathematical Finance* series strikes just the right balance between mathematical rigour and practical application.

Existing books on the challenging subject of stochastic interest rate models are often too advanced for Master's students or fail to include practical examples. *Stochastic Interest Rates* covers practical topics such as calibration, numerical implementation and model limitations in detail. The authors provide numerous exercises and carefully chosen examples to help students acquire the necessary skills to deal with interest rate modelling in a real-world setting. In addition, the book's webpage at www.cambridge.org/9781107002579 provides solutions to all of the exercises as well as the computer code (and associated spreadsheets) for all numerical work, which allows students to verify the results.

DARAGH MCINERNEY is a Director at the Valuation Modelling and Methodologies Group at UBS, and a researcher in mathematical finance at AGH University of Science and Technology in Kraków, Poland. He holds a PhD in Applied Mathematics from the University of Oxford, and has worked since 2001 as a quantitative analyst in both investment banking and fund management.

TOMASZ ZASTAWNIAK holds the Chair of Mathematical Finance at the University of York. He has authored about 50 research publications and six books. He has supervised four PhD dissertations and around 80 MSc dissertations in mathematical finance.

Mastering Mathematical Finance

Mastering Mathematical Finance is a series of short books that cover all core topics and the most common electives offered in Master's programmes in mathematical or quantitative finance. The books are closely coordinated and largely self-contained, and can be used efficiently in combination but also individually.

The MMF books start financially from scratch and mathematically assume only undergraduate calculus, linear algebra and elementary probability theory. The necessary mathematics is developed rigorously, with emphasis on a natural development of mathematical ideas and financial intuition, and the readers quickly see real-life financial applications, both for motivation and as the ultimate end for the theory. All books are written for both teaching and self-study, with worked examples, exercises and solutions.

[DMFM]   *Discrete Models of Financial Markets,*
            Marek Capiński, Ekkehard Kopp

[PF]   *Probability for Finance,*
            Ekkehard Kopp, Jan Malczak, Tomasz Zastawniak

[SCF]   *Stochastic Calculus for Finance,*
            Marek Capiński, Ekkehard Kopp, Janusz Traple

[BSM]   *The Black–Scholes Model,*
            Marek Capiński, Ekkehard Kopp

[PTRM]   *Portfolio Theory and Risk Management,*
            Maciej J. Capiński, Ekkehard Kopp

[NMFC]   *Numerical Methods in Finance with C++,*
            Maciej J. Capiński, Tomasz Zastawniak

[SIR]   *Stochastic Interest Rates,*
            Daragh McInerney, Tomasz Zastawniak

[CR]   *Credit Risk,*
            Marek Capiński, Tomasz Zastawniak

[SCAF]   *Stochastic Control Applied to Finance,*
            Szymon Peszat, Tomasz Zastawniak

Series editors Marek Capiński, *AGH University of Science and Technology, Kraków*; Ekkehard Kopp, *University of Hull*; Tomasz Zastawniak, *University of York*

Stochastic Interest Rates

DARAGH MCINERNEY
AGH University of Science and Technology, Kraków, Poland

TOMASZ ZASTAWNIAK
University of York, UK

CAMBRIDGE
UNIVERSITY PRESS

University Printing House, Cambridge CB2 8BS, United Kingdom

Cambridge University Press is part of the University of Cambridge.

It furthers the University's mission by disseminating knowledge in the pursuit of
education, learning and research at the highest international levels of excellence.

www.cambridge.org
Information on this title: www.cambridge.org/9781107002579

First published 2015

A catalogue record for this publication is available from the British Library

ISBN 978-1-107-00257-9 Hardback

To our daughters Teresa, Francesca, Karolina and Klementyna

Contents

Preface

In this volume of the 'Mastering Mathematical Finance' series we relax the assumption of constant interest rates adopted in the binomial or the Black–Scholes market models covered in earlier volumes, in particular [DMFM] and [BSM]. In general, interest rates are time dependent and random. Being closely linked to, and indeed determined by, fixed-income instruments traded in the market, the rates also depend on the maturity dates of the underlying instruments. This gives rise to the notion of term structure, i.e. the family of interest rates parameterised by the maturity date. We are going to study models describing the random evolution through time of the term structure, that is, of the entire family of interest rates for various maturities.

Because the rates for different maturities are related to one another and evolve simultaneously in time, their joint evolution is more intricate than that of a single quantity such as a stock price. There is not a single term structure model universally adopted as a benchmark to play a similar role as the Black–Scholes model does for stock prices. Instead, a range of alternative and to some extent complementary models are in use to capture various aspects of the evolution of the term structure. A selection of such models will be presented along with the associated interest rate derivative securities.

The prerequisites for this book are covered in some other volumes of the 'Mastering Mathematical Finance' series. These include probability theory [PF], stochastic calculus [SCF], and the Black–Scholes model [BSM]. Familiarity with Monte Carlo simulations [NMFC] will also be helpful.

We begin with various fundamental notions and properties associated with fixed-income instruments in Chapter 1 and the basic 'vanilla' interest rate derivatives in Chapter 2. Here we also cover the change of numeraire technique and introduce the notion of forward measure, a very useful alternative to the risk-neutral measure when pricing interest rate derivatives.

A number of short-rate models, in which the evolution of the entire term structure is driven by a single interest rate, namely the short rate, are covered in Chapter 3. In particular, the Merton, Vasiček and one-factor and two-factor Hull–White models are discussed in detail. In Chapter 4 we turn our attention to one-factor and multi-factor models of forward rates within what is known as the Heath–Jarrow–Morton (HJM) framework, and learn how the term structure is driven by the evolution of the family of forward rates.

Chapters 5, 6 and 7 are devoted to the LIBOR market model (LMM) and the swap market model (SMM). These models are presented and analysed in Chapter 5. In particular, Black's formula is derived for caplets and swaptions. This formula is essential for calibration to implied market volatilities, discussed in Chapter 6 along with the implementation of the LMM via Monte Carlo simulation. In Chapter 7 we introduce a range of options that can be valued within the LMM. Chapter 8 on modelling volatility skews and smiles concludes the volume.

The book contains a considerable number of examples and exercises, which are an important part of the course. The code and spreadsheets that were used to compute many of the numerical examples and plot some of the figures, along with the solutions to all exercises in this volume can be downloaded from www.cambridge.org/9781107002579.

1

Fixed-income instruments

At its simplest, an interest rate is the rate that is charged or paid for the use of money. It is often expressed as an annual percentage of the notional amount. Throughout the text we will generally focus on what are known as 'interbank rates'. These are the interest rates at which banks borrow from and lend to each other in the interbank, or over-the-counter (OTC) market. The most important example of an interbank rate is the London Interbank Offered Rate, or LIBOR. The LIBOR rate is the interest rate at which banks offer to lend unsecured funds to each other in the London wholesale money market. Another related market rate is the swap rate, which is the fixed rate that a bank is willing to exchange for a series of payments based on the LIBOR rate.

In this chapter we present some basic terminology and definitions, together with an overview of fixed-income instruments such as forward rate agreements (FRAs), swaps, floating-rate notes and fixed-coupon bonds. Government-backed securities form another important class of interest rate instruments. In the USD market, securities such as Treasury bonds, Treasury notes and Treasury bills are issued by the US Treasury to finance government debt. All instruments are assumed to be default free, that is, we do not account for the possibility that the issuers may fail to honour their commitments.

We begin with the definition of the zero-coupon bond. Such bonds are not actively traded within the interbank market. The reason they are important, however, is because interbank interest rates such as LIBOR and swap rates can be defined in terms of zero-coupon bonds. The set of zero-coupon bonds for various time horizons is known as the zero-coupon curve. How the zero-coupon curve is estimated from market data such as LIBOR and swap rates is also discussed.

In this chapter, and indeed throughout this volume, time is measured in years.

1.1   Interest rates and bonds

A **zero-coupon bond** or **discount bond** with maturity date T is a financial contract that guarantees the holder one dollar at time T. The bond can be thought of as the value at time $t < T$ of one dollar to be paid at time T. The zero-coupon bond maturing at time T is often referred to as a T-bond, and its price at time t is denoted by $B(t, T)$. Therefore, a zero-coupon bond is parameterised by two time indices, the current time t and the maturity date T. By definition, $B(T, T) = 1$, and we have

$$0 < B(t, T) < 1$$

for $t < T$.

The dependence of $B(t, T)$ on the maturity date T is known as the **term structure of discount factors** or **zero-coupon curve** at time t. The curve is a decreasing function of maturity.

Spot interest rates

Having defined the zero-coupon bond $B(t, T)$, we now introduce the notion of the simply compounded interest rate. The **simply compounded spot rate** at time t for maturity T is defined as the annualised rate of return from holding the bond from time t until maturity T. It is denoted by $L(t, T)$, and is defined as

$$L(t, T) = \frac{1 - B(t, T)}{(T - t)B(t, T)}. \tag{1.1}$$

The bond price $B(t, T)$ can be expressed in terms of the spot rate $L(t, T)$ as

$$B(t, T) = \frac{1}{1 + (T - t)L(t, T)}. \tag{1.2}$$

If interest rates are positive, we must have

$$B(t, S) > B(t, T)$$

for $t \leq S < T$.

An important example of a simply compounded rate is the **London Interbank Offered Rate** (**LIBOR**). This is the interest rate at which banks offer to lend unsecured funds to each other in the London wholesale money market. From now on we shall identify $L(t, T)$ with the LIBOR rate.

Remark 1.1
LIBOR is the primary benchmark for short-term interest rates. Daily fixings of LIBOR are published by the British Bankers Association (BBA) shortly after 11 a.m. (GMT). It is a filtered average of quotes provided by a number of banks and can be thought of as representing the lowest real-world cost of unsecured funding in the London money market. It is produced for ten major currencies, Pound Sterling, US Dollar, Euro, Japanese Yen, Swiss Franc, Canadian Dollar, Australian Dollar, Swedish Krona, Danish Krona and the New Zealand Dollar. Fifteen maturities are quoted for each currency ranging from overnight to 12 months. LIBOR rates are widely used as a reference rate for a range of vanilla financial instruments such as forward rate agreements, short-term interest rate futures contracts and interest rate swaps.

The Euro Interbank Offered Rate (EURIBOR) is another example of a money-market rate and is compiled by the European Banking Federation. The EURIBOR rate is the benchmark rate for EUR-denominated instruments.

Remark 1.2
We defined the simply compounded spot rate at time t as the rate of return over the interval $[t, T]$; see (1.1). For the case of USD LIBOR, however, the accrual period starts two London business days after time t (the date on which the rate becomes fixed). For example, for the six-month USD LIBOR spot rate on 15 March 2010 the accrual period begins on 17 March 2010 and ends on 17 September 2010. These timing conventions differ from currency to currency. Interest is calculated on an Actual/360 basis (see Remark 1.6). Throughout the text we will assume that spot rates fix and start on the same date, unless explicitly stated otherwise.

Interest rates quoted in the market are almost always simply compounded. However, it can be mathematically more convenient to work with continuously compounded rates. The **continuously compounded spot rate** is the annualised logarithmic rate of return from holding the bond from time t until maturity T. It is denoted by $R(t, T)$, and is defined as

$$R(t, T) = -\frac{\ln B(t, T)}{T - t}.$$

The zero-coupon bond price can be expressed in terms of $R(t, T)$ as

$$B(t, T) = e^{-R(t,T)(T-t)}. \tag{1.3}$$

The continuously compounded spot rate can be thought of as a measure of the implied interest rate offered by the bond and is sometimes referred to as the **yield to maturity**. The graph of $R(t, T)$ versus maturity T is known as the **yield curve** (see Figures 1.1 and 1.2). Yield curves are typically increasing or decreasing functions of T, but can often be inverted or 'hump' shaped.

Exercise 1.1   Consider an annually compounded spot rate $L(0, T)$ maturing in one year, i.e. $T = 1$. Compute the continuously compounded spot rate $R(0, T)$ when $L(0, T) = 5\%$.

Time value of money

The above definitions express the principle that today's value of one dollar paid at some time in the future is less than one dollar paid today. This is known as the **time value of money**.

A closely related notion is **discounted value** or **present value** (**PV**). It is the value today of a deterministic (known in advance) future payment or a series of deterministic future payments. We use the discount bond to express the present value. For example, an amount A known at time t to be paid at time $T > t$ has present value $B(t, T)A$ at time t.

The present value of a deterministic payment should not be confused with the more general concept of the discounted value of a random future payment. If we have a random payment X at some future time $T > t$, its discounted value $B(t, T)X$ at time t is also a random variable, whose value may be unknown at time t.

Exercise 1.2   Consider a perpetual bond that pays one dollar at the end of each year forever. Assuming that $B(0, T) = (1 + r)^{-T}$, where r is a constant annually compounded rate of interest, show that the present value of the perpetual bond, that is, the sum of the present values of all the payments, can be written as a geometric series. Simplify the series to find the present value of the perpetual bond for $r = 5\%$.

The bond price is a stochastic process

If the bond price were deterministic, then the following would have to be true.

Proposition 1.3
Let $t < S < T$. If the zero-coupon bond price $B(S,T)$ were known at time t (i.e. deterministic), then in the absence of arbitrage we would have

$$B(t,T) = B(t,S)B(S,T). \qquad (1.4)$$

Proof Suppose that $B(t,T) < B(t,S)B(S,T)$. Consider this strategy.
• At time t we buy (go long) a T-bond and sell (go short) an amount $B(S,T)$ of S-bonds to give an income of $B(t,S)B(S,T) - B(t,T) > 0$.
• At time S our short position in S-bonds matures and we are required to pay the amount $B(S,T)$. We raise this amount by selling one T-bond.
• At time T our net position will be zero. The long position in T-bonds purchased at time t cancels the short position in T-bonds purchased at time S.
Our strategy created a risk-free profit of $B(t,S)B(S,T) - B(t,T) > 0$ at time t, violating the no-arbitrage assumption. By adopting the opposite strategy, we can see that the reverse inequality $B(t,T) > B(t,S)B(S,T)$ would also give rise to an arbitrage opportunity.   □

If we were to perform an empirical analysis of a bond price time series, it would quickly become apparent that condition (1.4) is not satisfied. The zero-coupon bond price should therefore be modelled as a stochastic process that evolves towards a known value at time T.

1.2 Forward rate agreements

Let $t < S < T$. A **forward rate agreement** (**FRA**) is a contract entered into at time t, when the issuer agrees to pay the holder at time T the LIBOR rate $L(S,T)$ in exchange for a fixed rate K applied to a notional amount N. The value of the payoff at time T is given by

$$\tau(K - L(S,T))N, \qquad (1.5)$$

where $\tau = T - S$ is the accrual period. Without loss of generality, we can assume a unit notional, $N = 1$. By definition, it costs nothing to enter into a FRA. Taking the time t value of the cash flows described above and setting the resulting sum equal to zero, we can find the value of the fixed rate K such that the FRA is zero. The time t value of the fixed interest payment τK is simply the discounted value $\tau K B(t, T)$. The time t value of the floating payment is given by the following result.

Proposition 1.4
The arbitrage-free value at time t of the LIBOR-based payment $\tau L(S, T)$ at time T is $B(t, S) - B(t, T)$.

Proof To see this consider the following strategy.
- At time t we buy (go long) an S-bond and sell (go short) a T-bond.
- At time S the long position in S-bonds matures to yield one dollar. Use this income to buy an amount $1/B(S, T)$ of T-bonds.
- At time T our net position will be $\dfrac{1}{B(S, T)} - 1$, which is equal to $\tau L(S, T)$.

We have replicated the payment at time T using a self-financing strategy with an initial cost of $B(t, S) - B(t, T)$. In the absence of arbitrage this must be the value of the floating payment at time t. □

The value of the FRA at time t is therefore

$$B(t, T)\tau K - B(t, S) + B(t, T).$$

Setting this equal to zero and solving for K, we find that the value of the fixed rate, known as the **forward LIBOR rate** or simply the **forward rate** and denoted by $F(t; S, T)$, is

$$F(t; S, T) = \frac{B(t, S) - B(t, T)}{\tau B(t, T)}. \tag{1.6}$$

The forward rate is a simply compounded rate parameterised by three time arguments: the present time t, the start of the spot LIBOR rate $S > t$ and the maturity date $T > S$.

Exercise 1.3 Consider two annually compounded spot rates $L(0, S)$ and $L(0, T)$, maturing in one and two years respectively, i.e. $S = 1$ and $T = 2$. Compute $L(0, T)$ when $L(0, S) = 4\%$ and the forward rate $F(0; S, T) = 5.5\%$.

Exercise 1.4 For two annually compounded spot rates $L(0, 1) = 4\%$ and $L(0, 2) = 5\%$, maturing in one and two years respectively, compute the one-year to two-year forward rate $F(0; 1, 2)$.

1.3 Forward interest rates and forward bond price

Assume we wish to enter into an agreement at time t to purchase a T-bond at time S, where $t < S < T$. One of the simplest ways of determining the correct (arbitrage-free) amount A known at time t that we need to pay at time S is to take the time t value of the cash flows and set the resulting sum equal to zero,

$$-AB(t, S) + B(t, T) = 0.$$

The arbitrage-free amount we need to pay at time S to purchase the T-bond is known as the **forward bond price** or **forward discount factor**. It is denoted by $\mathbf{FP}(t; S, T)$ and given by

$$\mathbf{FP}(t; S, T) = \frac{B(t, T)}{B(t, S)}. \tag{1.7}$$

By rearranging (1.6), it can be seen that the forward bond price can be expressed in terms of the forward rate as

$$\mathbf{FP}(t; S, T) = \frac{B(t, T)}{B(t, S)} = \frac{1}{1 + (T - S)F(t; S, T)}.$$

Therefore, we can think of the forward rate as the simply compounded rate of return over the time interval $[S, T]$ implied by the forward bond price.

We can quote forward rates as either simple rates or continuously compounded rates. The **continuously compounded forward rate** at time t for expiry S and maturity T is denoted by $R(t; S, T)$. It is found by solving

$$\frac{B(t, T)}{B(t, S)} = e^{-R(t; S, T)(T - S)}. \tag{1.8}$$

The above can be written as

$$R(t; S, T) = -\frac{\ln B(t, T) - \ln B(t, S)}{T - S}.$$

Using (1.3), we can write this in terms of the continuously compounded spot rates as

$$R(t; S, T) = \frac{R(t, T)(T - t) - R(t, S)(S - t)}{T - S}.$$

Exercise 1.5 Given a continuously compounded spot rate $R(0, 1) = 4\%$ and a continuously compounded forward rate $R(0, 1, 2) = 5.5\%$, compute the spot rate $R(0, 2)$.

Remark 1.5

The forward rate $F(t; S, T)$ could be taken as a predictor of the actual spot interest rate $L(S, T)$ at time S. Indeed, $F(t; S, T)$ is the expectation of $L(S, T)$ under what is known as the T-forward measure (see Section 2.4 for more details).

Instantaneous rates

The **instantaneous forward rate** at time t for maturity T, which we denote by $f(t, T)$, can be thought of as the rate of return over an infinitesimally small time interval $[T, T + \delta T]$ or, more precisely,

$$f(t, T) = \lim_{\delta T \to 0} R(t, T, T + \delta T) = -\frac{\partial \ln B(t, T)}{\partial T}. \qquad (1.9)$$

The dependence of $f(t, T)$ on the maturity T is known as the **term structure of forward rates** (or **forward curve**) at time t.

A related concept is the **instantaneous short rate** or **risk-free rate** at time t, denoted by $r(t)$. It is the rate of return over the infinitesimal time interval $[t, t + \delta t]$, and is defined in terms of the instantaneous forward rate as

$$r(t) = f(t, t).$$

Although they are abstract concepts, the instantaneous forward and short rates play an important role in stochastic interest rate modelling. In Chapter 3 we cover models based on the short rate and then in Chapter 4 we study the seminal Heath–Jarrow–Morton model of the dynamics of the term structure of forward rates.

Bond price formula

Integrating (1.9) over the time interval $[t, T]$, we can see that

$$\int_t^T f(t, u)du = -\ln B(t, u)\Big|_t^T = -\ln B(t, T). \qquad (1.10)$$

Hence the zero-coupon bond price can be expressed in terms of the instantaneous forward rates as

$$B(t, T) = \exp\left(-\int_t^T f(t, u)du\right). \qquad (1.11)$$

Exercise 1.6 Show that the instantaneous forward rate $f(t, T)$ and the continuously compounded spot rate $R(t, T)$ are related by

$$f(t, T) = R(t, T) + (T - t)\frac{\partial}{\partial T}R(t, T).$$

Remark 1.6

In the expression for the simply compounded forward rate the interest accrues over the time interval $[S, T]$. In reality, however, how interest accrues over time is determined by **day-count conventions**. There are three main cases.

- Actual/365: assume there are 365 days in a year, and calculate the actual number of days between the dates and divide by 365.
- 30/360: assume there are 30 days in a month and 360 days in a year, and calculate the number of days accordingly and divide by 360.
- Actual/360: assume there are 360 days in a year, and calculate the actual number of days between the dates and divide by 360.

For the market LIBOR rates the accrual basis is Actual/360.

Example 1.7

Consider a three-month USD LIBOR rate beginning on 17 March 2010 and maturing three months later on 17 June 2010. The accrual period is $92/360 = 0.255\,55$.

1.4   Money market account

The **money market account** is a risk-free security where interest accrues
continuously at the instantaneous short rate $r(t)$. The short rate is typically
modelled as a stochastic process with the assumption that almost all sample
paths are Lebesgue integrable. The value of the money market account at
time t is denoted by $B(t)$, and is defined by the differential equation

$$dB(t) = r(t)B(t)dt$$

with $B(0) = 1$. Solving, we have

$$B(t) = \exp\left(\int_0^t r(u)du\right).$$

The money market account can be thought of as the amount earned by
starting with a unit amount at time 0 and continually reinvesting it at the
short rate $r(t)$ over the infinitesimal time interval $[t, t + \delta t]$. The money
market account is often referred to as the bank-account numeraire.

1.5   Coupon-bearing bonds

A **fixed-coupon bond** is a financial instrument that pays the holder deterministic (known at time $t \leq T_0$) amounts $c_1, \ldots, c_n$, referred to as **coupon
payments,** at times $T_1, \ldots, T_n$, where $T_0 < T_1 < \cdots < T_n$. At maturity,
time T_n, the holder receives the notional or face value N in addition to
the final coupon c_n. Computing the price of a fixed-coupon bond is simply a matter of discounting each cash flow back to time t. The value of a
fixed-coupon bond at time $t \leq T_0$, which we denote by $\mathbf{B}_{\text{fixed}}(t)$, is given by

$$\mathbf{B}_{\text{fixed}}(t) = \sum_{i=1}^{n} c_i B(t, T_i) + NB(t, T_n). \tag{1.12}$$

Coupons are typically quoted in terms of a fixed annualised rate of return K, known as the **coupon rate**. Each coupon is then defined as $c_i =
\tau_i NK$ for $i = 1, \ldots, n$, where $\tau_i = T_i - T_{i-1}$.

A **floating-coupon bond** or **floating-rate note** is analogous to a fixed-
coupon bond with the important difference that the coupon payment at time
T_i for $i = 1 \ldots, n$ is a function of the spot LIBOR rate $L(T_{i-1}, T_i)$, which is
unknown (stochastic) at time $t < T_{i-1}$. For $i = 1, \ldots, n$ the coupon payment

c_i at time T_i is

$$c_i = \tau_i NL(T_{i-1}, T_i) = N\left(\frac{1}{B(T_{i-1}, T_i)} - 1\right),$$

where $\tau_i = T_i - T_{i-1}$.

By Proposition 1.4, in the absence of arbitrage the time t value of the floating coupon payment at time T_i is $N(B(t, T_{i-1}) - B(t, T_i))$. The value at time t of the floating-coupon bond, which we denote by $\mathbf{B}_{\text{floating}}(t)$, is therefore

$$\mathbf{B}_{\text{floating}}(t) = N \sum_{i=1}^{n} (B(t, T_{i-1}) - B(t, T_i)) + NB(t, T_n)$$
$$= NB(t, T_0). \tag{1.13}$$

Note that, at time T_0, the value of the floating-coupon bond is equal to its notional, $\mathbf{B}_{\text{floating}}(T_0) = N$. In such cases the bond is said to be trading **at par**.

Exercise 1.7 The table below lists some 1-month GBP LIBOR rates from the period between January and June 2010.

i	T_{i-1}	T_i	$L(T_{i-1}, T_i)$
1	4 Jan 2010	1 Feb 2010	0.516 25%
2	1 Feb 2010	1 Mar 2010	0.519 38%
3	1 Mar 2010	1 Apr 2010	0.540 00%
4	1 Apr 2010	4 May 2010	0.547 50%
5	4 May 2010	1 Jun 2010	0.554 69%
6	1 Jun 2010	1 Jul 2010	0.565 94%

What was the cash flow of a floating-coupon bond starting at time T_0 and maturing at T_6 with six coupons payable at times $T_1, \ldots, T_6$ and face value 100 GBP?

1.6 Interest rate swaps

An **interest rate swap** is an OTC instrument in which two counterparties exchange a set of payments at a fixed rate of interest for a set of payments at a floating rate, typically the spot LIBOR rate. If the holder is paying the floating rate and receiving the fixed rate, the swap is said be a **receiver swap**. Alternatively, if the holder is receiving the floating rate and paying the fixed rate, the swap is called a **payer swap**.

Consider a unit notional amount $N = 1$ and a set of dates $T_0 < T_1 < \cdots < T_n$ with accrual periods $\tau_i = T_i - T_{i-1}$ for $i = 1, \ldots, n$. At time T_i, $i = 1, \ldots, n$, the holder of a payer swap pays a fixed amount $\tau_i K$, where K is a preassigned fixed rate of interest, the **swap rate**, in exchange for a floating payment of $\tau_i L(T_{i-1}, T_i)$, where $L(T_{i-1}, T_i)$ is the spot LIBOR fixing at time T_{i-1} for the ith accrual period. The number of payments n is referred to as the **length of the swap**, the payment dates $T_1, \ldots, T_n$ as the **settlement dates**, and the dates $T_0, \ldots, T_{n-1}$ as the **reset dates**. The first reset date T_0 is called the **start date** of the swap. If current time $t < T_0$, the swap agreement is referred to as a **forward-starting** payer or receiver swap.

Applying Proposition 1.4, we can see that the value at time $t \leq T_i$ of the time T_i floating payment is $B(t, T_{i-1}) - B(t, T_i)$. The value at time $t \leq T_0$ of the forward payer swap is therefore

$$
\begin{aligned}
\mathbf{PS}(t) &= \sum_{i=1}^{n} (B(t, T_{i-1}) - B(t, T_i)) - K \sum_{i=1}^{n} \tau_i B(t, T_i) \\
&= (B(t, T_0) - B(t, T_n)) - K \sum_{i=1}^{n} \tau_i B(t, T_i).
\end{aligned}
\tag{1.14}
$$

From the above expression it can be seen that the payer swap can be expressed as the difference between the floating-coupon bond (1.13) and the fixed-coupon bond (1.12),

$$
\mathbf{PS}(t) = \mathbf{B}_{\text{floating}}(t) - \mathbf{B}_{\text{fixed}}(t).
$$

The **forward swap rate**, denoted by $S_{0,n}(t)$, is the value of the fixed rate K that makes the time t value of the forward swap zero. Equivalently, it is the value of K that makes the time t value of the floating-coupon bond equal to that of the fixed-coupon bond. This gives

$$
S_{0,n}(t) = \frac{B(t, T_0) - B(t, T_n)}{\sum_{i=1}^{n} \tau_i B(t, T_i)}.
\tag{1.15}
$$

The denominator is often referred to as the **swap annuity** or **level**.

The swap rate can be written in terms of the forward bond price (1.7) by dividing both the numerator and the annuity by $B(t, T_0)$,

$$S_{0,n}(t) = \frac{1 - \mathbf{FP}(t; T_0, T_n)}{\displaystyle\sum_{i=1}^{n} \tau_i \mathbf{FP}(t; T_0, T_i)}.$$

The above formulae for the swap rate are often expressed in terms of the forward rates $F(t, T_{i-1}, T_i)$ for $i = 1, \ldots, n$. To see this note that the time t value of $\tau_i L(T_{i-1}, T_i)$, the floating-rate payment at time T_i, can be written as $\tau_i F(t, T_{i-1}, T_i) B(t, T_i)$. The value at time $t \le T_0$ of the forward payer swap (1.14) can therefore be expressed in terms of the forward rates,

$$\mathbf{PS}(t) = \sum_{i=1}^{n} \tau_i F(t; T_{i-1}, T_i) B(t, T_i) - K \sum_{i=1}^{n} \tau_i B(t, T_i).$$

Setting the above formula equal to zero and rearranging, we can express $S_{0,n}(t)$ as the sum of weighted forward rates

$$S_{0,n}(t) = \sum_{i=1}^{n} w_i(t) F(t; T_{i-1}, T_i), \qquad (1.16)$$

where the weights $w_i(t)$ are given by

$$w_i(t) = \frac{\tau_i B(t, T_i)}{\displaystyle\sum_{j=1}^{n} \tau_j B(t, T_j)} = \frac{\tau_i \mathbf{FP}(t; T_0, T_i)}{\displaystyle\sum_{j=1}^{n} \tau_j \mathbf{FP}(t; T_0, T_j)}.$$

Remark 1.8
We have expressed the swap rate in terms of zero-coupon bond prices. In reality, however, swap rates are traded benchmark securities, which we can use to determine the zero-coupon curve. In the next section we use a collection of **spot-starting** or **co-initial** swap rates, i.e. swap rates with various maturities that share the same start date, to build a zero-coupon curve by a method known as bootstrapping.

Remark 1.9
In the above description of the interest rate swap, the fixed and floating payments occur on the same dates. In reality, for a USD swap, fixed-payment dates or coupon dates are typically semiannual, and the floating-payment dates are quarterly, corresponding to the three-month spot LIBOR. Moreover, interest accrues on a 30/360 basis on the fixed leg and an Actual/360 basis on the floating leg.

Exercise 1.8 Using the data in the table below, compute the swap rate starting in one year with four semiannual payments over a two-year period.

Maturity T_i	$B(0, T_i)$
0.5	0.9756
1	0.9518
1.5	0.9286
2	0.9060
2.5	0.8839
3	0.8623

Exercise 1.9 Consider a set of dates $0 = T_0 < T_1 < \cdots < T_n$. Given a set of co-initial swap rates $S_{0,i}(0)$ for $i = 1, \ldots, n$, show how to iteratively solve for the discount factors $B(0, T_i)$.

1.7 Yield curve construction

In this section we examine how to calculate the zero-coupon curve, or equivalently the yield curve, from market data. We use a set of spot-starting swap rates to derive an approximation of the forward curve, that is, the term structure of forward rates $f(t, T)$ for $T > t$, where t is the current date (the spot date).

The problem of computing the forward curve from a finite set of swap rates is somewhat ill posed mathematically, as we do not have enough market data to uniquely determine the forward curve. We need to employ some form of interpolation. The assumptions we make, therefore, will play a role in determining the curve.

There are a number of possible interpolation schemes. The most common is that the instantaneous forward rates are taken to be constant between the maturities of the swap contracts. Therefore, the forward curve at time t will be approximated by a piecewise constant function.

The approximation for the forward curve can then be used to determine the zero-coupon curve via the bond-pricing equation (1.11) and the yield curve from (1.3). The resulting yield curve will be continuous but non-differentiable.

Yield curve from swap rates

We are given a sequence of co-initial interest rate swaps starting at the spot date t and such that $T_0, \ldots, T_{n_i-1}$ are the reset dates and T_{n_i} is the maturity date for the ith swap, where $t \le T_0 < T_1 < \cdots$ and where the lengths of the swaps form an increasing sequence $n_1 < n_2 < \cdots$. We denote the accrual periods by $\tau_j = T_j - T_{j-1}$ for $j = 1, 2, \ldots$.

The value on the spot date t of a spot-starting swap is zero. Hence, by (1.15),

$$B(t, T_0) - B(t, T_{n_i}) = r_i \sum_{j=1}^{n_i} \tau_j B(t, T_j) \tag{1.17}$$

for each $i = 1, 2, \ldots$, where the ith swap rate is denoted by $r_i = S_{0, n_i}(t)$ to keep the notation simple.

We adopt the piecewise constant interpolation of the instantaneous forward rate

$$f(t, T) = \begin{cases} f_1 & \text{for } t \le T \le T_{n_1}, \\ f_{i+1} & \text{for } T_{n_i} < T \le T_{n_{i+1}}, \, i = 1, 2, \ldots. \end{cases}$$

By (1.11), for $i = 1$ and $j = 0, \ldots, n_1$ we have

$$B(t, T_j) = \exp\left(-\int_t^{T_j} f(t, u) du\right) = \exp(-f_1(T_j - t)),$$

and can write (1.17) as

$$\exp(-f_1(T_0 - t)) - \exp(-f_1(T_{n_1} - t)) = r_1 \sum_{j=1}^{n_1} \tau_j \exp(-f_1(T_j - t)).$$

We then solve for f_1 using a root-finding algorithm such as the bisection or Newton–Raphson methods (see, for example, [NMFC]).

For the ith forward rate f_i an iterative procedure can be set up as follows. Suppose we have calculated the forward curve out to the maturity T_{n_i} of the ith swap. We now determine the constant forward rate f_{i+1} from time T_{n_i} to the next swap rate maturity $T_{n_{i+1}}$. We can write (1.17) as

$$B(t, T_{n_{i+1}}) + r_{i+1} \sum_{j=n_i+1}^{n_{i+1}} \tau_j B(t, T_j) = B(t, T_0) - r_{i+1} \sum_{j=1}^{n_i} \tau_j B(t, T_j).$$

Table 1.1 *USD swap rates on 18 May 2011.*

Length n_i	Swap rate r_i	Maturity T_{n_i}	Forward rate f_i
1	0.003 70	21 May 2012	0.003 6774
2	0.007 42	20 May 2013	0.011 1694
3	0.012 05	20 May 2014	0.021 4233
4	0.016 49	20 May 2015	0.030 1666
5	0.020 56	20 May 2016	0.037 5366
7	0.026 78	21 May 2018	0.043 7546
10	0.032 40	20 May 2021	0.047 8592
12	0.034 80	22 May 2023	0.049 7284
15	0.037 15	20 May 2026	0.049 9878
20	0.038 92	20 May 2031	0.046 8864
25	0.039 79	20 May 2036	0.045 6238
30	0.040 25	20 May 2041	0.044 6587

By (1.11), for $j = n_i + 1, \ldots, n_{i+1}$ we have

$$B(t, T_j) = \exp\left(-\int_t^{T_j} f(t, u)du\right) = B(t, T_{n_i}) \exp\left(-\int_{T_{n_i}}^{T_j} f(t, u)du\right)$$

$$= B(t, T_{n_i}) \exp(-f_{i+1}(T_j - T_{n_i})),$$

so we get

$$\exp(-f_{i+1}(T_{n_{i+1}} - T_{n_i})) + r_{i+1} \sum_{j=n_i+1}^{n_{i+1}} \tau_j \exp(-f_{i+1}(T_j - T_{n_i}))$$

$$= B(t, T_{n_i})^{-1} \left(B(t, T_0) - r_{i+1} \sum_{j=1}^{n_i} \tau_j B(t, T_j) \right).$$

The bond prices $B(t, T_j)$ are known for $j = 0, \ldots, n_i$ if the forward curve has already been computed up to maturity T_{n_i}, and the last equation can be solved for f_{i+1} by using a root-finding algorithm once again.

Example 1.10
We use a set of spot-starting (co-initial) swap rates listed in Table 1.1 with maturities $1, 2, 3, 4, 5, 7, 10, 12, 15, 20, 25, 30$ years and based on USD LIBOR to build the forward curve out to 30 years.

By convention, the start date T_0 of such a swap is two business days after the spot date t. The swaps pay interest on dates that use the same modified

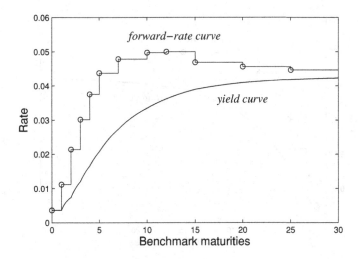

Figure 1.1 Instantaneous forward-rate curve $f(t, T)$ and yield curve $R(t, T)$ from swap rates in Example 1.10.

following-business-day conventions as USD LIBOR rates. If the maturity date of the LIBOR rate does not fall on a business day, then the next business day will be used unless that business day extends into a next calendar month, in which case the business day that precedes the maturity date is used. The floating-payment dates are quarterly (every three months) to correspond to a three-month LIBOR, and the fixed-payment dates (coupon dates) are semiannual (every six months). Interest is computed on an Actual/360 day basis on the floating side of the swap, and on a 30/360 day basis on the fixed side.

For the data in Table 1.1 the spot date t is 18 May 2011 and the start date T_0 is 20 May 2011 for each of the swap rates. The maturities are 21 May 2012 for the first swap, 20 May 2013 for the second swap, and so on.

In Figure 1.1 we plot the piecewise constant approximation to the instantaneous forward-rate curve derived form swap rates on 18 May 2011 as given in Table 1.1. The maturity dates for the spot swap rates are marked by circles. The (smooth) yield curve resulting from the forward-rate curve is also shown.

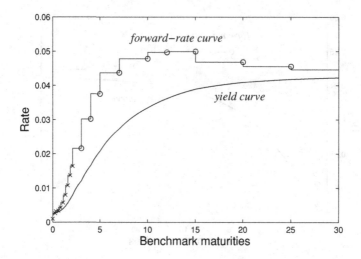

Figure 1.2 Instantaneous forward-rate curve $f(t, T)$ and yield curve $R(t, T)$ from LIBOR rates, futures prices and swap rates on 18 May 2011; see Remark 1.11.

Remark 1.11

To keep the discussion simple, we have used just the spot-starting swap rates with the understanding that the short-end of the yield curve will be poorly approximated.

In practice, the data sets employed to calibrate the yield curve also include LIBOR rates and futures prices, along with swap rates. The piecewise approximation to the instantaneous forward-rate curve and the corresponding yield curve computed for such market data on 18 May 2011 are shown in Figure 1.2. LIBOR deposits are used for the first three months before moving to Eurodollar futures. The first eight quarterly futures contracts are highly liquid and are used to build the curve from between three months to two years. After two years we change from Eurodollar futures to spot-starting swaps beginning with the three-year rate. The maturity dates for LIBOR rates and Eurodollar futures are marked by crosses, while the maturity dates for the spot swap rates are indicated by circles.

The short end of the curve in Figure 1.2 will better approximate the actual interest rate term structure implied by the market as compared to Figure 1.1. Forward rates calculated at the change-over point from futures to swaps can often display large jumps or discontinuities.

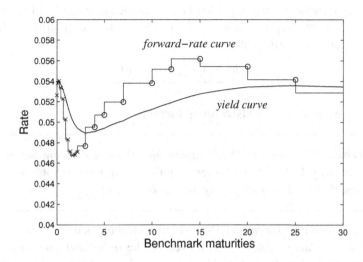

Figure 1.3 Instantaneous forward-rate curve $f(t, T)$ and yield curve $R(t, T)$ from LIBOR rates, futures prices and swap rates on 18 Apr 2007; see Remark 1.12.

Remark 1.12

Changes in the market due to the credit crisis have considerably complicated the construction of the yield curve. The LIBOR rate is the market rate for unsecured lending, therefore the credit worthiness of the counterparty becomes relevant. Though historically quite low, this credit-risk premium became important in the wake of the credit crisis. This makes the construction of the short end of the curve difficult. Indeed, it is now standard practice to construct a range of different yield curves rather than just one unique curve.

For comparison purposes, in Figure 1.3 we show the instantaneous forward rate computed from market data on 18 Apr 2007. This was just a few months before the start of the credit crisis. Here we can see that the yield curve is much flatter than in Figure 1.2.

Bootstrapping the swap rates

Rather than calculating the instantaneous forward rates, where we need to employ a numerical root-finding scheme, we can estimate a set of discount factors by using a simple bootstrapping technique along with an interpolation scheme.

We begin by noting that equation (1.17) can be rearranged so that the discount bond at swap-rate maturity T_{n_i} can be expressed in terms of the discount bonds on earlier dates,

$$B(t, T_{n_i}) = \frac{B(t, T_0) - \sum_{j=1}^{n_i-1} r_i \tau_j B(t, T_j)}{1 + \tau_{n_i} r_i}. \tag{1.18}$$

This is an example of a **bootstrapping formula**.

Exercise 1.10   Using (1.18), compute the prices of discount bonds with maturity 1, 2, 3, 4 and 5 years from the swap rates in Table 1.1. Assume that $t = T_0$ for simplicity, so that $B(t, T_0) = 1$.

The bootstrapping formula (1.18) gives the discount bond prices $B(t, T_{n_i})$ on the swap maturity dates T_{n_i}. However, on the right-hand side we also need the bond prices $B(t, T_j)$ on the dates T_j, and some of these dates may fall between the swap maturity dates. The standard approach to this problem is to perform a cubic spline interpolation between the benchmark maturities so that we get a swap rate for each T_j.

Example 1.13
For USD interest rate swaps we are typically working with a set of spot-starting swap rates with maturities 1, 2, 3, 4, 5, 7, 10, 12, 15, 20, 25 and 30 years. But we also need the swap rates for each annual maturity between these dates. In Figure 1.4 the market swap rates from Table 1.1 are indicated by circles and the interpolated ones by crosses.

We can compare the discount factors calculated by this approach with those in Example 1.10 by plotting the discount curve implied by the forward curve shown in Figure 1.2. This is done in Figure 1.5. As we can see, the agreement, though not exact, is reasonable.

The key advantage of this approach is that it is computationally very fast. In Chapter 5 on the LIBOR market model we will use the bootstrapping formula (1.18) to calculate a set of discount factors and hence LIBOR rates between two dates; see Example 5.8.

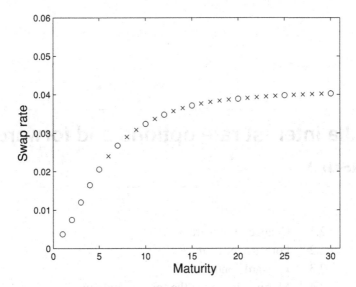

Figure 1.4 Market swap rates (circles) and interpolated swap rates (crosses) for data in Table 1.1; see Example 1.13.

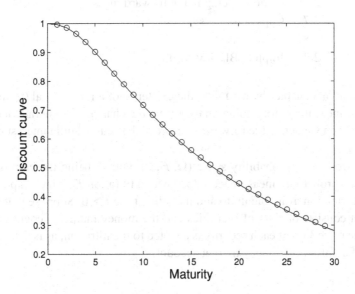

Figure 1.5 Discount curve $B(t, T)$ implied by the yield curve in Figure 1.1 (solid line) and discount bond prices computed by bootstrapping with interpolation (circles); see Example 1.13.

2

Vanilla interest rate options and forward measure

We begin this chapter by assuming the existence of a risk-neutral (or martingale) measure, before going on to present the change of numeraire technique. Then we define the forward measure and discuss vanilla interest rate options.

We work on a probability space $(\Omega, \mathcal{F}, P)$, with P being the empirical (market) probability measure, equipped with a filtration $\mathcal{F}_t$, which captures the information available up to and including time $t \geq 0$. Suppose that the market consists of a set of securities and the money market account such that the price $V(t)$ of each security is adapted to the filtration, as is the price $B(t)$ of a unit of the money market account.

Assumption 2.1

There exists a probability measure Q equivalent to P such that the price $V(t)$ of any security discounted by $B(t)$ is a martingale under Q, that is, for any $0 \leq t < T$

$$\mathbb{E}_Q\left(\frac{V(T)}{B(T)}\middle| \mathcal{F}_t\right) = \frac{V(t)}{B(t)}. \tag{2.1}$$

We say that Q is a **risk-neutral measure** or **martingale measure**. This assumption is closely linked to the absence of arbitrage.

2.1 Change of numeraire

In the context of stochastic interest rates the risk-neutral measure Q is generally difficult to work with. In contrast to the Black–Scholes framework, the money market account is now stochastic. For example, consider a payoff at time T that depends on a LIBOR rate $L(S, T)$, where $t < S \leq T$, such as the FRA covered in Chapter 1. The FRA payoff at time T is $\tau(K - L(S, T))$, where $\tau = T - S$ is the accrual period of the LIBOR rate. Under the risk-neutral measure Q, the value of the FRA at time $t < S$ is

$$V(t) = B(t)\mathbb{E}_Q\left(B(T)\tau(K - L(S, T))|\mathcal{F}_t\right).$$

To calculate this expectation we need to model the joint probability distribution of the money market account $B(T)$ and the LIBOR rate $L(S, T)$. This can be avoided and replaced by the distribution of a single random variable under a suitable choice of measure.

When changing from one measure to another, a key concept is that of a **numeraire**, defined as any traded asset that pays no dividends and whose price $A(t)$ is positive at any time $t \geq 0$. The money market account $B(t)$ is an example of a numeraire.

Proposition 2.2
For any choice of numeraire $A(t)$ and for any $T > 0$ there is a probability measure P_A equivalent to Q such that the price $V(t)$ of any security discounted by $A(t)$ becomes a martingale under P_A in the time interval $[0, T]$, that is,

$$\mathbb{E}_{P_A}\left(\frac{V(T)}{A(T)}\middle| \mathcal{F}_t\right) = \frac{V(t)}{A(t)} \quad \text{for} \quad 0 \leq t \leq T.$$

Proof According to Assumption 2.1, since the numeraire is a tradeable security, its price $\frac{A(t)}{B(t)}$ discounted by the money market account is a martingale under the risk-neutral measure Q. It follows that

$$\mathbb{E}_Q\left(\frac{A(T)}{B(T)}\right) = \frac{A(0)}{B(0)}.$$

As a result,

$$Z = \frac{B(0)}{A(0)}\frac{A(T)}{B(T)}$$

is a positive random variable such that $\mathbb{E}_Q(Z) = 1$. This enables us to define a probability measure P_A by taking Z as its density (Radon–Nikodym derivative) with respect to Q,

$$\frac{dP_A}{dQ} = Z.$$

Since $Z > 0$, it follows that P_A is equivalent to Q and $\frac{dQ}{dP_A} = \frac{1}{Z}$ is also an integrable random variable under Q.

We know that for any security its discounted price $\frac{V(t)}{B(t)}$ is a martingale under Q. This means, in particular, that $\frac{V(T)}{B(T)}$ is integrable under Q, which in turn implies that the random variable

$$\frac{V(T)}{A(T)} = \frac{B(0)}{A(0)}\frac{V(T)}{B(T)}\frac{1}{Z}$$

is integrable under P_A, and the Bayes formula for conditional expectation

$$\mathbb{E}_{P_A}\left(\frac{V(T)}{A(T)}\bigg|\mathcal{F}_t\right) = \frac{\mathbb{E}_Q\left(\frac{dP_A}{dQ}\frac{V(T)}{A(T)}\bigg|\mathcal{F}_t\right)}{\mathbb{E}_Q\left(\frac{dP_A}{dQ}\bigg|\mathcal{F}_t\right)} \tag{2.2}$$

holds for any t such that $0 \le t \le T$; see [PF]. Observe that

$$\mathbb{E}_Q\left(\frac{dP_A}{dQ}\bigg|\mathcal{F}_t\right) = \frac{B(0)}{A(0)}\mathbb{E}_Q\left(\frac{A(T)}{B(T)}\bigg|\mathcal{F}_t\right) = \frac{B(0)}{A(0)}\frac{A(t)}{B(t)}$$

because $\frac{A(t)}{B(t)}$ is a martingale under Q. Futhermore,

$$\mathbb{E}_Q\left(\frac{dP_A}{dQ}\frac{V(T)}{A(T)}\bigg|\mathcal{F}_t\right) = \frac{B(0)}{A(0)}\mathbb{E}_Q\left(\frac{V(T)}{B(T)}\bigg|\mathcal{F}_t\right) = \frac{B(0)}{A(0)}\frac{V(t)}{B(t)}$$

since $\frac{V(t)}{B(t)}$ is a martingale under Q. It follows that

$$\mathbb{E}_{P_A}\left(\frac{V(T)}{A(T)}\bigg|\mathcal{F}_t\right) = \frac{V(t)}{A(t)},$$

completing the proof.   □

Exercise 2.1 Show that the time 0 price of a European derivative security with payoff X and exercise time $T > 0$ can be written as

$$V(0) = A(0)\mathbb{E}_{P_A}\left(\frac{X}{A(T)}\right),$$

irrespective of the choice of numeraire A.

We have seen in the proof of Proposition 2.2 that the **Radon–Nikodym derivative** of P_A with respect to Q is given by

$$\frac{dP_A}{dQ} = \frac{B(0)}{A(0)}\frac{A(T)}{B(T)}. \tag{2.3}$$

The **Radon–Nikodym density process** is defined as

$$\left.\frac{dP_A}{dQ}\right|_t = \mathbb{E}_Q\left(\left.\frac{dP_A}{dQ}\right|\mathcal{F}_t\right)$$

for $0 \le t \le T$. It is clearly a martingale under Q, and

$$\left.\frac{dP_A}{dQ}\right|_t = \mathbb{E}_Q\left(\left.\frac{B(0)}{A(0)}\frac{A(T)}{B(T)}\right|\mathcal{F}_t\right) = \frac{B(0)}{A(0)}\frac{A(t)}{B(t)}.$$

We frequently switch between different numeraires when working with stochastic interest rates, which distinguishes this case from the Black–Scholes setting, where typically the money market account plays the role of numeraire. A popular choice of numeraire is the zero-coupon bond. The associated measure is known as the forward measure.

2.2 Forward measure

Consider the price at time t of a European derivative security with time T payoff X. It is given by the usual valuation formula

$$V(t) = B(t)\mathbb{E}_Q\left(\left.\frac{X}{B(T)}\right|\mathcal{F}_t\right). \tag{2.4}$$

To calculate the expectation we need to evaluate the joint distribution of the stochastic money market account $B(T)$ and the random payoff X. A simpler and more natural way of computing the above expectation is to use the zero-coupon T-bond $B(t, T)$ as numeraire.

The measure associated with the choice of $B(t, T)$ as numeraire is called the **forward measure** for settlement date T, and will be denoted by P_T.

It is a probability measure equivalent to Q defined on the σ-field $\mathcal{F}_T$ with Radon–Nikodym derivative

$$\frac{dP_T}{dQ} = \frac{B(0)}{B(0,T)} \frac{B(T,T)}{B(T)} = \frac{1}{B(T)B(0,T)}. \tag{2.5}$$

The Radon–Nikodym density process is

$$\left.\frac{dP_T}{dQ}\right|_t = \mathbb{E}_Q\left(\left.\frac{1}{B(T)B(0,T)}\right|\mathcal{F}_t\right) = \frac{B(t,T)}{B(t)B(0,T)} \tag{2.6}$$

for $0 \le t \le T$, where clearly $\left.\frac{dP_T}{dQ}\right|_0 = 1$.

Exercise 2.2 Show that

$$\frac{dP_S}{dP_T} = \frac{B(0,T)}{B(0,S)} \frac{1}{B(S,T)} \quad \text{when } S \le T,$$

and

$$\frac{dP_S}{dP_T} = \frac{B(0,T)}{B(0,S)} B(T,S) \quad \text{when } S \ge T.$$

The price at time t of the time T payoff X can be written as

$$V(t) = B(t,T)\mathbb{E}_{P_T}\left(\left.\frac{X}{B(T,T)}\right|\mathcal{F}_t\right) = B(t,T)\mathbb{E}_{P_T}(X|\mathcal{F}_t). \tag{2.7}$$

This is consistent with Exercise 2.1 for $t = 0$. What have we gained? Instead of the joint distribution of X and $B(T)$ under Q, all we need to know is the distribution of X under P_T.

To derive an explicit expression for the change of measure we make the assumption that $B(t,T)$ obeys the SDE

$$dB(t,T) = B(t,T)r(t)dt + B(t,T)\Sigma(t,T)dW(t), \tag{2.8}$$

where $W(t)$ is standard Brownian motion under the risk-neutral measure Q, and $r(t)$ is the instantaneous short rate. By definition, $B(T,T) = 1$.

Exercise 2.3 Suppose that

$$dB(t,T) = B(t,T)\mu(t,T)dt + B(t,T)\Sigma(t,T)dW(t),$$

where $W(t)$ is standard Brownian motion under the risk-neutral measure Q. Show that $\mu(t,T) = r(t)$ for each $t \in [0,T]$.

Exercise 2.4 Solve the SDE (2.8) for $B(t, T)$ with the final condition $B(T, T) = 1$.

We can apply the Itô formula to show that the Radon–Nikodym density process $\xi(t) = \left.\frac{dP_T}{dQ}\right|_t$ given by (2.6) satisfies the SDE

$$d\xi(t) = \xi(t)\Sigma(t, T)dW(t). \tag{2.9}$$

Exercise 2.5 Show that the Radon–Nikodym density process does indeed satisfy (2.9).

Solving SDE (2.9) for $\xi(t)$ with the initial condition $\xi(0) = 1$, we obtain

$$\xi(t) = \left.\frac{dP_T}{dQ}\right|_t = \exp\left(\int_0^t \Sigma(u, T)dW(u) - \frac{1}{2}\int_0^t \Sigma(u, T)^2 du\right).$$

For $t = T$ this gives the Radon–Nikodym derivative of P_T with respect to Q.

Proposition 2.3
If the zero-coupon bond price $B(t, T)$ obeys the SDE (2.8), then

$$\frac{dP_T}{dQ} = \exp\left(\int_0^T \Sigma(u, T)dW(u) - \frac{1}{2}\int_0^T \Sigma(u, T)^2 du\right).$$

Exercise 2.6 Suppose that $B(t, T)$ satisfies the SDE

$$dB(t, T) = B(t, T)r(t)dt + B(t, T)\sum_{i=1}^{n}\Sigma_i(t, T)dW_i(t),$$

where the $W_i(t)$ are independent standard Brownian motions under the risk-neutral measure Q for $i = 1, \ldots, n$. Derive a formula for $\frac{dP_T}{dQ}$ in terms of $\Sigma_i(t, T)$ and $W_i(t)$.

2.3 Forward contract

Consider a forward contract where we agree to buy an asset on some future delivery date T for an amount $F(t, T)$ determined at time $t < T$. The forward price $F(t, T)$ is such that the value of the forward contract, denoted by $V(t)$, is zero at time t. The cash flow at time T is $X(T) - F(t, T)$, where $X(T)$ is the asset price. The value of the forward contract at time t is

$$V(t) = B(t, T)\mathbb{E}_{P_T}(X(T) - F(t, T)|\mathcal{F}_t) = 0.$$

Since $F(t, T)$ is an $\mathcal{F}_t$-measurable random variable, the forward price is

$$F(t, T) = \mathbb{E}_{P_T}(X(T)|\mathcal{F}_t) \tag{2.10}$$

for any $t \in [0, T]$. Therefore the forward price is a martingale under P_T. In other words, the forward price can be regarded as an unbiased estimator of $X(T)$, where the expectation is taken under the forward measure.

2.4   Martingales under the forward measure

Recall the definition of the forward bond price $\mathbf{FP}(t; S, T)$ in Chapter 1. It is the price set at time t to be paid at time S for a zero-coupon T-bond. By (2.10), the forward price can be expressed as

$$\mathbf{FP}(t; S, T) = \mathbb{E}_{P_S}(B(S, T)|\mathcal{F}_t) = \mathbb{E}_{P_S}\left(\left.\frac{B(S, T)}{B(S, S)}\right|\mathcal{F}_t\right) = \frac{B(t, T)}{B(t, S)}.$$

The above is a specific instance of the general principle that the price of any non-dividend-paying tradeable asset divided by a numeraire is a martingale under the measure associated with the numeraire. This is a consequence of Proposition 2.2. In the case under consideration the numeraire is the S-bond.

Another example of a martingale under the forward measure is the forward rate. By (1.6),

$$F(t; S, T) = \frac{1}{\tau}\left(\frac{B(t, S)}{B(t, T)} - 1\right),$$

where $\tau = T - S$. The simply compounded forward rate $F(t; S, T)$ is a martingale under the forward measure P_T.

For $t = S$ the forward rate $F(S; S, T)$ is the spot LIBOR rate $L(S, T)$. Via the martingale property we have

$$F(t; S, T) = \mathbb{E}_{P_T}(L(S, T)|\mathcal{F}_t) \tag{2.11}$$

for each $t \in [0, S]$. The forward rate at time t can be regarded as an unbiased estimator of the future spot LIBOR rate under the forward measure P_T.

2.5 FRAs and interest rate swaps: the forward measure

In Chapter 1 we derived the value of an FRA by using a portfolio replication argument. Here we derive the same expression by valuing the cash flow at maturity under the appropriate forward measure. A payment at time T based on the spot LIBOR rate $L(S, T)$ is exchanged for a payment based on a fixed rate K. The cash flow at time T is $\tau(K - L(S, T))$, where $\tau = T - S$ is the accrual period of the spot LIBOR rate. The fixed rate K is the rate chosen so that the value $V(t)$ of the FRA is zero at time t. Under the forward measure P_T the value of the FRA is

$$V(t) = B(t, T)\mathbb{E}_{P_T}(\tau(K - L(S, T))|\mathcal{F}_t) = 0.$$

Using the martingale property (2.11) and the fact that K is $\mathcal{F}_t$-measurable, we can simplify the above expression to

$$V(t) = B(t, T)\tau K - B(t, T)\tau F(t; S, T) = 0.$$

Therefore the fixed rate is the forward rate, $K = F(t; S, T)$.

Formula (1.14) for the forward payer swap can also be derived by using forward measures. Consider a unit notional amount and a set of dates $T_0 < T_1 < \cdots < T_n$ with accrual periods $\tau_i = T_i - T_{i-1}$ for $i = 1, \ldots, n$. At time T_i the holder of the payer swap pays a fixed amount $\tau_i K$ in exchange for a floating payment of $\tau_i L(T_{i-1}, T_i)$. The value at time t of the cash flow can be evaluated as

$$\mathbf{PS}(t) = \sum_{i=1}^{n} B(t, T_i)\mathbb{E}_{P_{T_i}}(\tau_i(L(T_{i-1}, T_i) - K)|\mathcal{F}_t)$$

$$= \sum_{i=1}^{n} B(t, T_i)\tau_i(F(t; T_{i-1}, T_i) - K)$$

$$= B(t, T_0) - B(t, T_n) - K\sum_{i=1}^{n} \tau_i B(t, T_i),$$

where we use the fact that the forward rate $F(t, T_{i-1}, T_i)$ is a martingale under the forward measure P_{T_i}.

2.6 Option pricing in the forward measure

We now apply the techniques developed in this chapter to price a European option written on a zero-coupon bond. If we assume that, for each $T > 0$, the zero-coupon bond $B(t, T)$ follows the SDE (2.8) with a deterministic

$\Sigma(t, T)$, which means that $B(t, T)$ is log-normally distributed, then we can derive a Black–Scholes-type formula for the option price.

Let us consider a call option with expiry time S and strike K written on a zero-coupon bond $B(t, T)$, where $0 < S < T$. At any time $t < S$ the option can be priced as

$$V(t) = B(t)\mathbb{E}_Q\left(\frac{(B(S, T) - K)^+}{B(S)}\middle|\mathcal{F}_t\right)$$

$$= B(t)\mathbb{E}_Q\left(\frac{B(S, T)}{B(S)}\mathbf{1}_{\{B(S,T)\geq K\}}\middle|\mathcal{F}_t\right) - KB(t)\mathbb{E}_Q\left(\frac{1}{B(S)}\mathbf{1}_{\{B(S,T)\geq K\}}\middle|\mathcal{F}_t\right),$$

where $\{B(S, T) \geq K\}$ is the exercise set. Using Proposition 2.2, we can change the numeraire to $B(t, T)$ in the first expectation in the last line, and to $B(t, S)$ in the second expectation. This gives

$$V(t) = B(t, T)\mathbb{E}_{P_T}\left(\{\mathbf{1}_{\{B(S,T)\geq K\}}\middle|\mathcal{F}_t\right) - KB(t, S)\mathbb{E}_{P_S}\left(\mathbf{1}_{\{B(S,T)\geq K\}}\middle|\mathcal{F}_t\right)$$

$$= B(t, T)P_T(B(S, T) \geq K|\mathcal{F}_t) - KB(t, S)P_S(B(S, T) \geq K|\mathcal{F}_t).$$

$$(2.12)$$

To calculate these probabilities we need to know the distribution of $B(S, T)$ under P_T and also under P_S.

We begin with P_S. Recall that the forward bond price $\mathbf{FP}(t; S, T) = \frac{B(t,T)}{B(t,S)}$ is a martingale under P_S. Given that the bond prices follow (2.8), we can verify by means of the Itô formula that

$$d\mathbf{FP}(t; S, T) = \mathbf{FP}(t; S, T)(\Sigma(t, T) - \Sigma(t, S)) dW(t)$$

$$+ \mathbf{FP}(t; S, T)\Sigma(t, S)(\Sigma(t, S) - \Sigma(t, T)) dt. \quad (2.13)$$

Exercise 2.7   Show that the forward bond price process $\mathbf{FP}(t; S, T)$ satisfies the SDE (2.13).

From Proposition 2.3 we know that

$$\frac{dP_S}{dQ} = \exp\left(\int_0^S \Sigma(t, S)dW(u) - \frac{1}{2}\int_0^S \Sigma(u, S)^2 du\right).$$

Hence, by Girsanov's theorem (see [BSM]), the process

$$W^S(t) = W(t) - \int_0^t \Sigma(u, S)du \quad \text{for} \quad t \in [0, S] \quad (2.14)$$

is a Brownian motion under P_S. Because $\mathbf{FP}(t; S, T)$ is a martingale under P_S, there should be no dt term if we write $d\mathbf{FP}(t; S, T)$ in terms of

$dW^S(t)$ rather than $dW(t)$. Indeed, substituting $dW(t) = dW^S(t) + \Sigma(t, S) dt$ in (2.13), we obtain

$$d\mathbf{FP}(t; S, T) = \mathbf{FP}(t; S, T) (\Sigma(t, T) - \Sigma(t, S)) dW^S(t). \qquad (2.15)$$

Solving this linear SDE with $\mathbf{FP}(S; S, T) = B(S, T)$ gives

$$B(S, T) = \mathbf{FP}(t; S, T) \exp\left(\int_t^S (\Sigma(u, T) - \Sigma(u, S)) dW^S(u) \right.$$
$$\left. - \frac{1}{2} \int_t^S (\Sigma(u, T) - \Sigma(u, S))^2 du \right). \qquad (2.16)$$

Since $\Sigma(t, S)$ and $\Sigma(t, T)$ are deterministic and $W^S(t)$ is a Brownian motion under P_S, the expression in the exponent, which is equal to $\ln \frac{B(S,T)}{\mathbf{FP}(t;S,T)}$, is independent of $\mathcal{F}_t$ and normally distributed with variance

$$v(t, S) = \int_t^S (\Sigma(u, T) - \Sigma(u, S))^2 du$$

and mean $-\frac{1}{2} v(t, S)$ under P_S. Moreover, $\mathbf{FP}(t; S, T)$ is $\mathcal{F}_t$-measurable. It follows that

$$P_S \left(B(S, T) \geq K | \mathcal{F}_t \right) = N(d_-), \qquad (2.17)$$

where

$$N(x) = \frac{1}{\sqrt{2\pi}} \int_{-\infty}^x e^{-\frac{1}{2} y^2} dy$$

is the standard normal distribution function and

$$d_- = \frac{\ln \frac{\mathbf{FP}(t;S,T)}{K} - \frac{1}{2} v(t, S)}{\sqrt{v(t, S)}} = \frac{\ln \frac{B(t,T)}{K B(t,S)} - \frac{1}{2} v(t, S)}{\sqrt{v(t, S)}}. \qquad (2.18)$$

To compute the first probability in (2.12) we take

$$W^T(t) = W(t) - \int_0^t \Sigma(u, T) du \quad \text{for} \quad t \in [0, S],$$

which, by Proposition 2.3 and Girsanov's theorem, is a Brownian motion under P_T. Since

$$W^S(t) = W(t) - \int_0^t \Sigma(u, S) du = W^T(t) + \int_0^t (\Sigma(u, T) - \Sigma(u, S)) du,$$

substituting this into (2.16), we get

$$B(S,T) = \mathbf{FP}(t;S,T)\exp\left(\int_t^S (\Sigma(u,T) - \Sigma(u,S))\,dW^T(u)\right.$$

$$\left. + \frac{1}{2}\int_t^S (\Sigma(u,T) - \Sigma(u,S))^2\,du\right).$$

The expression in the exponent, which is equal to $\ln\frac{B(S,T)}{\mathbf{FP}(t;S,T)}$, is independent of $\mathcal{F}_t$ and normally distributed with mean $\frac{1}{2}v(t,S)$ and variance $v(t,S)$ under P_T. As a result,

$$P_T\,(B(S,T) \geq K|\mathcal{F}_t) = N(d_+), \tag{2.19}$$

where

$$d_+ = \frac{\ln\frac{\mathbf{FP}(t;S,T)}{K} + \frac{1}{2}v(t,S)}{\sqrt{v(t,S)}} = \frac{\ln\frac{B(t,T)}{KB(t,S)} + \frac{1}{2}v(t,S)}{\sqrt{v(t,S)}}. \tag{2.20}$$

Exercise 2.8   Verify (2.17) and (2.19) in detail using the fact that $\ln\frac{B(S,T)}{\mathbf{FP}(t;S,T)}$ is independent of $\mathcal{F}_t$ and normally distributed with mean $-\frac{1}{2}v(t,S)$ and variance $v(t,S)^2$ under P_S and with mean $\frac{1}{2}v(t,S)$ and variance $v(t,S)^2$ under P_T.

We have established the following result, similar to the classical Black–Scholes formula; see [BSM].

Theorem 2.4
If zero-coupon bonds follow the SDE (2.8) with deterministic log-volatility $\Sigma(t,T)$, then the time t price $\mathbf{BC}(t;S,T,K)$ of a call option with strike K and expiry S written on a zero-coupon bond with maturity T, where $0 \leq t < S < T$, is

$$\mathbf{BC}(t;S,T,K) = B(t,T)N(d_+) - KB(t,S)N(d_-) \tag{2.21}$$

with d_+, d_- given by (2.18) and (2.20), respectively.

We shall return to this formula again in Chapters 3 and 4, where we study some term structure models which yield an analytic formula for the zero-coupon bond price.

Put-call parity for bond options

We now use a replication argument to outline a put-call parity relationship for bond options. At time t consider a portfolio that consists of a long position in one call option, $\mathbf{BC}(t; S, T, K)$, and a short position in one put option, $\mathbf{BP}(t; S, T, K)$. Both options have strike K and expiry $S > t$, and are written on a zero-coupon bond with maturity $T > S$. The value at time S of this portfolio is

$$(B(S,T) - K)^+ - (K - B(S,T))^+ = B(S,T) - K.$$

It can be replicated by a portfolio consisting of a long position in one zero-coupon bond maturing at time T and a short position in K zero-coupon bonds maturing at time S. In the absence of arbitrage both portfolios must have the same value at time t, that is,

$$\mathbf{BC}(t; S, T, K) - \mathbf{BP}(t; S, T, K) = B(t, T) - KB(t, S).$$

This relation is known as **put-call parity** for bond options.

Exercise 2.9 Given formula (2.21) for the price of a call option, use put-call parity to derive the formula

$$\mathbf{BP}(t; S, T, K) = KB(t, S)N(-d_-) - B(t, T)N(-d_+) \qquad (2.22)$$

for the corresponding put option.

2.7 Caps and floors

An interest rate **cap** or **floor** can be thought of as an option on an interest rate (typically a spot LIBOR rate), or equivalently on a zero-coupon bond. Consider a unit notional amount and a set of dates $T_0 < T_1 < \cdots < T_n$ with accrual periods $\tau_i = T_i - T_{i-1}$ for $i = 1, \ldots, n$. At time T_i, where $i = 1, \ldots, n$, the holder of an interest rate cap or floor receives $\tau_i(L(T_{i-1}, T_i) - K)^+$ or $\tau_i(K - L(T_{i-1}, T_i))^+$, respectively, where K is a preassigned fixed rate, known as the **cap rate**.

The payment at time T_i for any $i = 1, \ldots, n$ is called a **caplet** or **floorlet**. The ith caplet is a European option with expiry T_i written on the spot LIBOR rate $L(T_{i-1}, T_i)$ with payoff

$$\tau_i(L(T_{i-1}, T_i) - K)^+. \qquad (2.23)$$

The payoff of the caplet becomes known at time T_{i-1} (when the LIBOR rate fixes), and it pays at time T_i.

In the following we show that an interest rate caplet is equivalent to a put option on a zero-coupon bond. We begin by noting that the caplet payoff (2.23) at time T_i is an $\mathcal{F}_{T_{i-1}}$-measurable random variable, and is therefore equivalent to the payoff

$$\tau_i B(T_{i-1}, T_i)(L(T_{i-1}, T_i) - K)^+$$

at time T_{i-1}. Using the definition (1.1) of the LIBOR rate $L(T_{i-1}, T_i)$, we can write this time T_{i-1} payoff as

$$(1 + \tau_i K)\left(\frac{1}{1 + \tau_i K} - B(T_{i-1}, T_i)\right)^+.$$

The caplet can be viewed as a portfolio of $1 + \tau_i K$ put options with strike $(1 + \tau_i K)^{-1}$ and expiry T_{i-1}, written on a zero-coupon bond with maturity T_i.

Summing the n caplets, we get the price at time t of the interest rate cap,

$$\mathbf{Cap}(t) = \sum_{i=1}^{n}(1 + \tau_i K)\mathbf{BP}\left(t; T_{i-1}, T_i, \frac{1}{1 + \tau_i K}\right),$$

where the formula for the zero-coupon bond put option is given by (2.22).

Similarly, we can show that the equivalent floorlet is a portfolio of $1 + \tau_i K$ call options with strike $(1 + \tau_i K)^{-1}$ and expiry T_{i-1}, written on a zero-coupon bond with maturity T_i. Again, summing the n floorlets, we find that the price at time t of the interest rate floor is

$$\mathbf{Flr}(t) = \sum_{i=1}^{n}(1 + \tau_i K)\mathbf{BC}\left(t; T_{i-1}, T_i, \frac{1}{1 + \tau_i K}\right),$$

with the zero-coupon bond call option price given by (2.21).

Example 2.5
Like interest rate swaps, caps and floors can either be spot or forward start-ing. For example, a 1-by-5 forward-starting cap consists of 16 caplets. The first caplet payoff becomes known one year from today and the last in four years and nine months. The contract matures in five years' time, when the last caplet is paid. Meanwhile, a seven-year spot-starting cap consists of 27 caplets and matures in seven years' time, when the last caplet is paid, with the first caplet payment becoming known in three months from today and the last in six years and nine months.

Put-call parity for caps and floors

At time t consider a portfolio that is long one cap, **Cap**(t), and short one floor, **Flr**(t), where both options have the same contractual features. At time T_i the cash flow from this portfolio is $\tau_i B(T_{i-1}, T_i)(L(T_{i-1}, T_i) - K)$. This is none other than the cash flow at time T_i for a payer swap. Therefore, at time t we can replicate the cash flows generated by the portfolio by entering into a forward-starting payer swap **PS**(t) with settlement dates $T_1, \ldots, T_n$ and swap rate K. This implies that

$$\mathbf{Cap}(t) - \mathbf{Flr}(t) = \mathbf{PS}(t).$$

2.8 Swaptions

Swaptions are European calls and puts on interest rate swaps. The expiry time of a swaption is typically the first reset date T_0 of the underlying interest rate swap. The holder of a **payer** (or **receiver**) **swaption** has the right to enter a payer (or receiver) swap at time T_0.

Example 2.6
A 2-into-5 year payer swaption with strike 3.5% gives the holder the right to enter a five-year payer swap starting in two years. That is, in two years' time the holder has the right (but not the obligation) to enter a five-year payer interest rate swap to receive a spot LIBOR floating rate in return for a fixed rate of 3.5%.

The length of the underlying interest rate swap (measured in years) is referred to as the **tenor**.

Consider a payer interest rate swap **PS**(t) with settlement dates $T_1, \ldots, T_n$ and reset dates $T_0, \ldots, T_{n-1}$. The payer swaption payoff is

$$\mathbf{PSwpt}_{0,n}(T_0) = (\mathbf{PS}(T_0))^+,$$

and its value at time t is given by

$$\mathbf{PSwpt}_{0,n}(t) = B(t)\mathbb{E}_Q\left(\frac{(\mathbf{PS}(T_0))^+}{B(T_0)} \,\middle|\, \mathcal{F}_t \right).$$

The underlying payer swap can be expressed in a number of different ways.

Using the results in Section 1.6, we have the price of the payer swap at the first reset date T_0 (the swaption expiry) given by

$$\mathbf{PS}(T_0) = \sum_{i=1}^{n} B(T_0, T_i)\tau_i(F(T_0; T_{i-1}, T_i) - K)$$

$$= 1 - B(T_0, T_n) - K \sum_{i=1}^{n} \tau_i B(T_0, T_i).$$

Hence the swaption can be thought of as a put option with strike 1 written on a coupon-bearing bond with coupon rate K. Furthermore, using formula (1.15) for the swap rate, we can write the payer swap as

$$\mathbf{PS}(T_0) = (S_{0,n}(T_0) - K) \sum_{i=1}^{n} \tau_i B(T_0, T_i).$$

It is clear that the payer swaption will be exercised if and only if the swap rate at expiry is greater than the strike.

Put-call parity for swaptions

There is a simple put-call parity relationship for swaptions. At time t, consider a portfolio that consists of a long position in one payer swaption and a short position in one receiver swaption. Both options have strike K and expiry T_0. The payoff at time T_0 for this portfolio is

$$(\mathbf{PS}(T_0))^+ - (-\mathbf{PS}(T_0))^+ = \mathbf{PS}(T_0).$$

Therefore, in the absence of arbitrage we must have, at time $t \leq T_0$,

$$\mathbf{PSwpt}_{0,n}(t) - \mathbf{RSwpt}_{0,n}(t) = \mathbf{PS}(t).$$

The difference between a payer swaption and a receiver swaption is equal to a forward-starting swap.

A swaption is said to be at-the-money when the strike rate K is equal to the forward swap rate $S_{0,n}(t)$. In this case the value of the forward-starting swap is zero, and by put-call parity the at-the-money payer swaption is equal to the at-the-money receiver swaption.

2.9 Implied Black volatility

Interest rate caps and floors can be expressed in terms of a series of caplets or floorlets. The market convention is to quote their prices as implied volatilities.

If the market quotes prices as implied volatilities, then how do we obtain the actual price? We need to use what is known as **Black's formula**. For the caplet payoff (2.23) at time T_i this formula reads

$$\mathbf{Cpl}_i^{\text{Black}}(t; \sigma) = \tau_i B(t, T_i)(F(t; T_{i-1}, T_i)N(d_+) - KN(d_-)), \qquad (2.24)$$

where

$$d_+ = \frac{\ln \frac{F(t;T_{i-1},T_i)}{K} + \frac{1}{2}\sigma^2(T_{i-1} - t)}{\sigma \sqrt{T_{i-1} - t}}, \qquad d_- = d_+ - \sigma \sqrt{T_{i-1} - t},$$

and where $F(t; T_{i-1}, T_i)$ is the simply compounded forward LIBOR rate. The **implied Black volatility** or **spot volatility** $\hat{\sigma}_i^{\text{caplet}}$ of the ith caplet is defined as the unique solution to the equation

$$\mathbf{Cpl}_i^{\text{mkt}}(t) = \mathbf{Cpl}_i^{\text{Black}}(t; \hat{\sigma}_i^{\text{caplet}}), \qquad (2.25)$$

where $\mathbf{Cpl}_i^{\text{mkt}}(t)$ is the caplet price derived from the quoted cap prices; see Remark 2.7.

For a cap with payment dates $T_1, \ldots, T_n$ the typical market convention is to assume that the same implied volatility is used for each caplet that constitutes the n-period cap. This volatility is denoted by $\hat{\sigma}_n^{\text{cap}}$ and referred to as the **flat volatility**. By definition, $\hat{\sigma}_n^{\text{cap}}$ solves the equation

$$\mathbf{Cap}^{\text{mkt}}(t) = \sum_{i=1}^{n} \mathbf{Cpl}_i^{\text{Black}}(t; \hat{\sigma}_n^{\text{cap}})$$

for the time t market price of the cap. The flat volatility is therefore the unique volatility that must be inserted into Black's formula for each caplet to obtain the market price of the cap.

For example, the flat volatility for various cap maturities on 18 May 2011 (post credit crisis) is presented in Figure 2.1. The set of flat volatilities for each cap maturity is referred to as the **volatility term structure**. Before the credit crisis the graph of the volatility term structure was typically hump shaped. The implied volatility would be upward sloping for maturities up to two or three years and would fall gradually for caps with a longer time to maturity. However, since the credit crisis the implied volatilities for short maturities have become very high relative to other maturities.

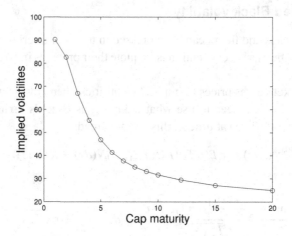

Figure 2.1 USD at-the-money flat volatility for different cap maturities on 18 May 2011.

Remark 2.7

The market quotes cap (floor) prices in terms of the flat volatility. The set of spot volatilities can be derived by applying a bootstrapping procedure to the set of flat volatilities quoted in the market.

Black's formula for swaptions

As is the case with caps (and floors), the swaption price is quoted in the market as an implied Black volatility. Black's formula for a T_0 into $T_n - T_0$ payer swaption written on a swap with settlement dates $T_1, \ldots, T_n$ and reset dates $T_0, \ldots, T_{n-1}$ as described in Section 2.8 reads

$$\mathbf{PSwpt}_{0,n}^{\mathrm{Black}}(t; \sigma) = \sum_{i=1}^{n} \tau_i B(t, T_i)(S_{0,n}(t)N(d_+) - KN(d_-)), \quad (2.26)$$

where

$$d_+ = \frac{\ln \dfrac{S_{0,n}(t)}{K} + \dfrac{1}{2}\sigma^2(T_0 - t)}{\sigma \sqrt{T_0 - t}}, \quad d_- = d_+ - \sigma \sqrt{T_0 - t},$$

with $S_{0,n}(t)$ being the swap rate. By definition, the **implied Black swaption volatility** $\hat{\sigma}_{0,n}^{\mathrm{swpt}}$ solves the equation

$$\mathbf{PSwpt}_{0,n}^{\mathrm{mkt}}(t) = \mathbf{PSwpt}_{0,n}^{\mathrm{Black}}(t; \hat{\sigma}_{0,n}^{\mathrm{swpt}})$$

Table 2.1 *At-the-money implied swaption volatilities for the USD market on 18 May 2011. The rows labelled 1y, ... ,30y denote the time to expiry of the swaption. The tenor of the underlying swap is given by the columns labelled 1y, ... ,20y.*

	1y	2y	3y	5y	7y	10y	15y	20y
1y	74.70	59.70	49.40	37.90	32.40	28.60	24.60	23.30
2y	51.90	43.50	38.10	32.20	29.10	26.60	23.70	22.60
3y	38.90	34.30	31.50	28.40	26.50	24.70	22.50	21.70
5y	27.50	26.40	25.60	24.50	23.50	22.40	20.70	20.30
10y	20.90	20.70	20.40	20.10	19.70	19.40	18.00	17.50
15y	18.10	18.10	18.10	18.00	17.90	17.50	16.00	15.80
20y	17.30	17.10	16.90	16.40	16.30	16.10	15.20	15.00
30y	17.40	17.40	17.10	16.60	16.70	17.00	16.70	17.00

for the market price of the swaption.

Example 2.8

In the market, at-the-money swaption prices are quoted as a grid of implied volatilities where one axis is the time to expiry and the other is the tenor of the underlying swap. See Table 2.1 for the at-the-money implied swaption volatilities for the USD market on 18 May 2011. We can see, for example, that on this date the implied volatility for the at-the-money 2-into-5 year payer swaption was 32.20%.

The market provides swaption volatilities only for certain standard maturities and tenors. If the volatility for 6-into-10 year swaptions is needed, then this will have to be inferred from the market quotes. To this end, market practitioners will take a set of quoted volatilities such as those in Table 2.1 and use interpolation to create a volatility surface such as that shown in Figure 2.2.

Remark 2.9

The Black formulae, which have been used since the 1970s, were motivated by Black's model for options on commodity futures, the key assumption being that the underlying variable follows a driftless log-normal process under some probability measure. It was not until the development of the LIBOR market model (LMM) in the late 1990s, however, that the Black

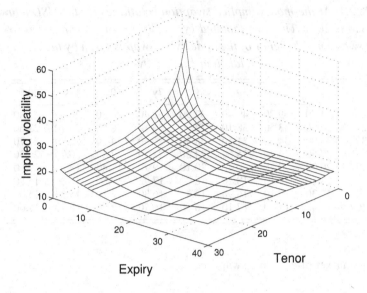

Figure 2.2 USD at-the-money implied swaption surface for 18 May 2011.

formula for caps was given a logically consistent theoretical basis. Likewise, Black's formula for swaptions can be derived within the framework
of the swap market model. We defer the derivation of Black's formulae
until Chapter 5.

Remark 2.10

An implicit assumption in Black's formula is that for a given underlying the
volatility is constant. In reality the volatility we need to insert into Black's
formula to match the market price varies with the strike price. For a given
swaption the graph of the implied volatility as a function of the strike K is
typically smile shaped. The strike price adds a 'third dimension' (in addition to the expiry and tenor) to the market quotes. Practitioners represent
this data as a three-dimensional matrix, called the **volatility cube**.

In the following chapters we cover a number of stochastic interest rate
models. To calibrate the parameters used in these models we need to use
prices in the vanilla market. Therefore the set of implied Black volatilities
quoted in the market (along with the interest rate term structure) play a key
role in specifying the model parameters.

3

Short-rate models

We need to choose a quantity to serve as a state variable that determines the interest rate term structure and its evolution in time. The first generation of stochastic interest rate models use the instantaneous short rate as the state variable. The two key advantages of short-rate models are their general simplicity and the fact that they often lead to analytic formulae for bonds and associated vanilla options. The tractability of short-rate models means that the price of a given derivative can often be computed quickly, important in situations where a large number of securities need to be valued. Indeed, throughout this chapter, we focus on short-rate models that allow discount bonds to be priced in closed form.

One-factor models assume that the entire interest rate term structure is driven by a one-dimensional Wiener process. Such models are usually suitable when pricing securities that depend on a single rate only, but for more complex products which depend on two or more different rates we may need to move to a multi-factor model driven by multi-dimensional Brownian motion. In the final section we present one of the most popular multi-factor short-rate models, the two-factor Hull–White model.

A weakness of the short-rate approach is that the instantaneous short rate is a mathematical idealisation rather than something that can be observed directly in the market. In the past decade, short-rate models have, to some extent, been superseded by the LIBOR market model (covered in Chapter 5), in which the stochastic state variable is a set of benchmark forward LIBOR rates. Nonetheless, short-rate models are particularly useful and remain popular due to their analytic tractability.

We continue to work under Assumption 2.1, which stipulates the existence of a probability measure Q (the risk-neutral measure) equivalent to P such that the value of any security discounted by the money market account is a martingale under Q.

3.1 General properties

In a **one-factor short-rate model** we assume that the short rate $r(t)$ satisfies an SDE of the form

$$dr(t) = \mu(t, r(t))dt + \sigma(t, r(t))dW(t), \qquad (3.1)$$

where $W(t)$ is a Brownian motion under the risk-neutral measure Q. We also assume that, for any $T \geq 0$, the price of the T-bond depends on the instantaneous short rate,

$$B(t, T) = F(t, r(t); T),$$

where $F(t, r; T)$ is a sufficiently smooth function to allow all transformations that follow.

Using Itô's formula to compute $dB(t, T) = dF(t, r(t), T)$, we can write

$$dB(t, T) = \alpha(t, T)B(t, T)dt + \Sigma(t, T)B(t, T)dW(t),$$

where

$$\alpha(t, T) = \frac{\frac{\partial F}{\partial t}(t, r(t); T) + \mu(t, r(t))\frac{\partial F}{\partial r}(t, r(t); T) + \frac{1}{2}\sigma(t, r(t))^2\frac{\partial^2 F}{\partial r^2}(t, r(t); T)}{F(t, r(t); T)},$$

$$\Sigma(t, T) = \frac{\sigma(t, r(t))\frac{\partial F}{\partial r}(t, r(t); T)}{F(t, r(t); T)}.$$

Since $W(t)$ is a Brownian motion under Q, from Exercise 2.3 we know that $\alpha(t, T) = r(t)$. This shows that $F(t, r; T)$ must satisfy the partial differential equation

$$\frac{\partial F}{\partial t} + \mu\frac{\partial F}{\partial r} + \frac{1}{2}\sigma^2\frac{\partial^2 F}{\partial r^2} = rF \qquad (3.2)$$

called the **term structure equation**. Because $B(T, T) = 1$, this equation

Table 3.1 *A selection of short-rate models.*

Model	$\mu(t, r(t))$	$\sigma(t, r(t))$
Merton	α	σ
Vasiček	$\theta - \alpha r(t)$	σ
Cox–Ingersoll–Ross	$\alpha(\beta - r(t))$	$\sigma \sqrt{r(t)}$
Dothan	$\alpha r(t)$	$\sigma r(t)$
Black–Derman–Toy	$\theta(t)r(t)$	$\sigma(t)r(t)$
Ho–Lee	$\theta(t)$	σ
Hull–White (extended Vasiček)	$\theta(t) - \alpha r(t)$	$\sigma(t)$
Black–Karasiński	$r(t)(\theta(t) - \alpha \ln r(t))$	$\sigma r(t)$

can be solved subject to the final condition $F(T, r; T) = 1$ to find a formula for $F(t, r; T)$ and hence for the bond price $B(t, T)$ for any $t < T$.

Nonetheless, we are going to adopt an alternative approach, utilising the fact that $\frac{B(t,T)}{B(t)}$ is a martingale under the risk-neutral measure Q and $B(t) = \exp\left(\int_0^t r(s)ds\right)$, so the bond price can be expressed as

$$B(t, T) = B(t)\mathbb{E}_Q\left(\frac{B(T,T)}{B(T)}\bigg|\mathcal{F}_t\right) = \mathbb{E}_Q\left(\exp\left(-\int_t^T r(s)ds\right)\bigg|\mathcal{F}_t\right). \quad (3.3)$$

3.2 Popular short-rate models

A number of models have been proposed for the dynamics of the short rate under the risk-neutral measure Q. These models specify a particular form for $\mu(t, r(t))$ and $\sigma(t, r(t))$. A list is shown in Table 3.1. It is not exhaustive, and various other possible functional forms for the risk-neutral drift and volatility can be proposed.

For the majority of models in Table 3.1 the short rate is either normally distributed (Merton, Vasiček, Ho–Lee and Hull–White) or log-normally distributed (Dothan, Black–Derman–Toy and Black–Krasiński). The Cox–Ingersoll–Ross model does not fit into either of these two categories as it features the non-central chi-squared distribution. Models where the short rate is normally distributed (Gaussian) are the most analytically tractable.

The model parameters are determined by calibrating to the current term structure of interest rates and to the implied volatilities of actively traded vanilla options (caps, floors and swaptions). However, on doing this calibration we quickly see that some of the models provide only an approximate fit to the present term structure of interest rates. This issue is discussed in more detail when we present the Vasiček model.

3.3 Merton model

This is arguably the simplest short-rate model. The SDE for the short rate is

$$dr(t) = \alpha dt + \sigma dW(t),$$

where α and σ are constants, and where $W(t)$ is a Brownian motion under the risk-neutral measure Q. This gives

$$r(s) = r(t) + \alpha(s - t) + \sigma(W(s) - W(t)).$$

We can see that the short rate is normally distributed.

The Merton model gives rise to a simple analytic formula for the bond price, which we derive below.

Bond pricing formula

Since the short rate is normally distributed, computing the expectation in (3.3) reduces to calculating the expected value of a log-normal random variable. Integrating between t and T, we have

$$\int_t^T r(s)ds = r(t)(T - t) + \frac{1}{2}\alpha(T - t)^2 + \sigma \int_t^T W(s)ds - \sigma W(t)(T - t).$$

Noting that

$$d\left((T - s)W(s)\right) = -W(s)ds + (T - s)dW(s),$$

we can replace the last two terms to get

$$\int_t^T r(s)ds = r(t)(T - t) + \frac{1}{2}\alpha(T - t)^2 + \sigma \int_t^T (T - s)dW(s).$$

It follows that

$$X = \frac{1}{2}\alpha(T - t)^2 + \sigma \int_t^T (T - s)dW(s)$$

is independent of $\mathcal{F}_t$ and normally distributed with mean $m = \frac{1}{2}\alpha(T - t)^2$ and variance $s^2 = \sigma^2 \int_t^T (T - s)^2 ds = \frac{1}{3}\sigma^2(T - t)^3$ under the risk-neutral measure Q. Because the expectation of e^{-X} is $e^{-m+\frac{1}{2}s^2}$, this proves the following result.

Proposition 3.1
The zero-coupon bond price in the Merton model can be expressed as

$$B(t,T) = \exp\left(-r(t)(T-t) - \frac{1}{2}\alpha(T-t)^2 + \frac{1}{6}\sigma^2(T-t)^3\right). \quad (3.4)$$

Proof By (3.3), since $r(t)$ is $\mathcal{F}_t$-measurable and X is independent of $\mathcal{F}_t$,

$$\begin{aligned}
B(t,T) &= \mathbb{E}_Q\left(\exp\left(-\int_0^T r(s)ds\right)\Big|\mathcal{F}_t\right) \\
&= \mathbb{E}_Q\left(\exp\left(-r(t)(T-t)\right)\exp\left(-X\right)\big|\mathcal{F}_t\right) \\
&= \exp\left(-r(t)(T-t)\right)\mathbb{E}_Q\left(\exp\left(-X\right)\right) \\
&= \exp\left(-r(t)(T-t) - m + \frac{1}{2}s^2\right) \\
&= \exp\left(-r(t)(T-t) - \frac{1}{2}\alpha(T-t)^2 + \frac{1}{6}\sigma^2(T-t)^2\right).
\end{aligned}$$

$\square$

Exercise 3.1 Let $B(t,T) = F(t,r(t);T)$ be the zero-coupon bond price (3.4) in the Merton model. Show that $F(t,r;T)$ satisfies the term structure equation (3.2).

3.4 Vasiček model

A problem with the Merton model is that the short rates can be negative, but an even more pressing issue is that it fails to model the dynamics correctly. An important empirical feature is that, when interest rates are high, there is a tendency for them to fall over time and, likewise, when the rates are low, they tend to rise. This is captured by the Vasiček model

$$dr(t) = (\theta - \alpha r(t))dt + \sigma dW(t),$$

where θ, α, σ are constants and $W(t)$ is a Brownian motion under the risk-neutral measure Q.

This is considered the first realistic model of the short rate. Vasiček modelled the short rate using a mean-reverting drift. The drift is positive when $r(t)$ is below θ/α, and negative when $r(t)$ is greater than θ/α.

The SDE for $r(t)$ can be solved explicitly. Observe that

$$d\left(e^{\alpha t}r(t)\right) = \theta e^{\alpha t}dt + \sigma e^{\alpha t}dW(t).$$

Integrating from t to time $s \geq t$, and multiplying both sides of the equality by $e^{-\alpha s}$, we get

$$r(s) = r(t)e^{-\alpha(s-t)} + \theta \int_t^s e^{-\alpha(s-u)}du + \sigma \int_t^s e^{-\alpha(s-u)}dW(u).$$

From the above we can see that the short rate is normally distributed under the risk-neutral measure Q with mean

$$\mathbb{E}_Q(r(s)) = r(0)e^{-\alpha s} + \theta \int_0^s e^{-\alpha(s-u)}du = r(0)e^{-\alpha s} + \theta\frac{1 - e^{-\alpha s}}{\alpha}$$

and variance given by the Itô isometry as

$$\text{Var}(r(s)) = \sigma^2 \int_0^s e^{-2\alpha(s-u)}du = \sigma^2\frac{1 - e^{-2\alpha s}}{2\alpha}.$$

As time s tends to infinity, the expectation of the short rate $r(s)$ tends to θ/α. The short rate is mean reverting. Moreover, because the short rate is normally distributed, it can become negative. This feature of the model might at first be considered a fatal flaw. Nonetheless, in practical applications the probability of the short rate becoming negative is often small.

Bond pricing formula

Computing the integral of $r(s)$ from t to T, we have

$$\int_t^T r(s)ds = r(t) \int_t^T e^{-\alpha(s-t)}ds$$

$$+ \theta \int_t^T \left(\int_t^s e^{-\alpha(T-u)}du\right)ds + \sigma \int_t^T \left(\int_t^s e^{-\alpha(T-u)}dW(u)\right)ds.$$

Let us denote the integral in the first term on the right-hand side by

$$D(t,T) = \int_t^T e^{-\alpha(s-t)}ds = \frac{1 - e^{-\alpha(T-t)}}{\alpha}. \tag{3.5}$$

To compute the second and third terms observe that

$$d\left(\int_t^s e^{-\alpha(s-u)}du\right) = ds - \alpha\left(\int_t^s e^{-\alpha(s-u)}du\right)ds,$$

$$d\left(\int_t^s e^{-\alpha(s-u)}dW(u)\right) = dW(s) - \alpha\left(\int_t^s e^{-\alpha(s-u)}dW(u)\right)ds.$$

Hence

$$\left(\int_t^s e^{-\alpha(s-u)}du\right)ds = d\left(\int_t^s \frac{1-e^{-\alpha(s-u)}}{\alpha}du\right)$$

$$= d\left(\int_t^s D(u,s)du\right),$$

$$\left(\int_t^s e^{-\alpha(s-u)}dW(u)\right)ds = d\left(\int_t^s \frac{1-e^{-\alpha(s-u)}}{\alpha}dW(u)\right)$$

$$= d\left(\int_t^s D(u,s)dW(u)\right).$$

As a result, integrating from t to T, we find that

$$\int_t^T r(s)ds = r(t)D(t,T) + \theta\int_t^T D(u,T)du + \sigma\int_t^T D(u,T)dW(u).$$

It follows that

$$X = \theta\int_t^T D(u,T)du + \sigma\int_t^T D(u,T)dW(u)$$

is a random variable independent of $\mathcal{F}_t$, normally distributed with mean

$$m = \theta\int_t^T D(u,T)du$$

and variance given by the Itô isometry as

$$s^2 = \sigma^2\int_t^T D(u,T)^2du$$

under the risk-neutral measure Q. The expectation of e^{-X} is $e^{-m+\frac{1}{2}s^2}$. Hence, using the bond pricing formula (3.3), we arrive at the following result just like in the proof of Proposition 3.1.

Proposition 3.2

The zero-coupon bond price in the Vasiček model can be expressed as

$$B(t,T) = \exp\left(- r(t)D(t,T) - \theta \int_t^T D(u,T)du \right.$$

$$\left. + \frac{1}{2}\sigma^2 \int_t^T D(u,T)^2 du \right), \qquad (3.6)$$

where $D(t,T)$ is given by (3.5).

Exercise 3.2 Compute the mean m and variance s^2 of X and hence express the bond price $B(t,T)$ in the Vasiček model explicitly in terms of the parameters θ, α, σ.

Exercise 3.3 Let $B(t,T) = F(t,r(t);T)$ be the zero-coupon bond price (3.6) in the Vasiček model. Show that $F(t,r;T)$ satisfies the term structure equation (3.2).

Remark 3.3

Note that, in both the Merton and Vasiček models, bond prices can be written as

$$B(t,T) = e^{f(t,T)-g(t,T)r(t)},$$

where $f(t,T)$ and $g(t,T)$ are deterministic functions. Models of this type are referred to as **affine term structure models**. The value of affine term structure models lies in their relative simplicity. In general, if the drift term $\mu(t,r(t))$ and the square of the volatility $\sigma(t,r(t))^2$ are affine functions of the short rate $r(t)$ in the SDE (3.1), that is, if

$$\mu(t,r(t)) = \gamma(t)r(t) + \delta(t), \qquad \sigma(t,r(t))^2 = \eta(t)r(t) + \epsilon(t),$$

where the time-dependent functions are suitably well behaved, then the model is said to possess an affine term structure. All models in Table 3.1 have this property, except for the Black–Derman–Toy, Black–Karasiński and Dothan models.

Table 3.2 *Calibration to zero-coupon bond prices implied by the USD interest rate curve on 18 May 2011 in Example 3.4.*

Maturity	$B^{mkt}(0,T)$	$B(0,T)$	% Error
1	0.9962	0.9943	0.00
2	0.9851	0.9803	0.01
3	0.9645	0.9594	0.03
4	0.9359	0.9329	0.06
5	0.9013	0.9020	0.10
6	0.8628	0.8678	0.14
7	0.8258	0.8315	0.18
8	0.7873	0.7936	0.22
9	0.7504	0.7550	0.26
10	0.7153	0.7163	0.29

Calibration

The model parameters are chosen to match the initial interest rate term structure. Suppose that, at time 0, we are given a set of N zero-coupon bond prices for $i = 1, \ldots, N$ derived from a set of actively traded benchmark securities. Denoting the analytic expression found in Exercise 3.2 for the bond prices in terms of the model parameters by $B(0, T_i; \theta, \alpha, \sigma)$, we can perform the least squares optimisation

$$\min_{\theta, \alpha, \sigma} \sum_{i=1}^{N} \left(B^{mkt}(0, T_i) - B(0, T_i; \theta, \alpha, \sigma) \right)^2 \tag{3.7}$$

to compute the parameter values for the best match between the model and market data.

However, as N is typically far greater than the number of model parameters (three in the Vasiček model), we find that after performing the optimisation the zero-coupon curve implied by the model often fails to accurately match that given by the market. This is particularly true when the market curve is inverted. It is a serious flaw in models such as Vasiček where we have only a limited number of constant parameters. In general, the current price of a zero-coupon T-bond given by the model will rarely match the market price. The model's failure to match even the current zero-coupon curve means it cannot be used for more exotic interest rate derivatives.

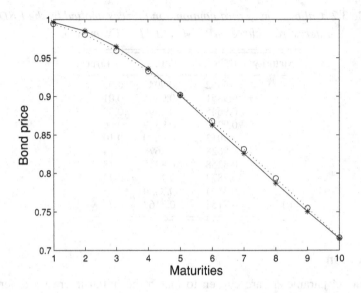

Figure 3.1 Results for least squares optimisation for market price data on 18 May 2011 in Example 3.4. The market-implied zero-coupon bond prices $B^{\mathrm{mkt}}(t, T)$ are indicated by asterisks, and the model prices $B(t, T)$ by circles.

Example 3.4

In this numerical example we calibrate to a set of bond prices in Table 3.2 derived from the interest rate curve on 18 May 2011. The parameters computed by least squares optimisation are $\theta = 0.0099, \alpha = 0.131, \sigma = 0.01$.

To check if the parameters are in any sense financially realistic we can consider the ratio θ/α, which is the expectation of the short rate as time tends to infinity. This value is 0.075 66, which is plausible. However, for the given set of parameters the model provides only an approximate match to the current discount curve, as can be seen in Figure 3.1.

3.5 Hull–White model

To reproduce exactly the initial zero-coupon curve we need a time-varying parameter. This parameter is specifically chosen to provide an exact match to the initial term structure. Arguably, the most popular model with time-dependent parameters is the Hull–White model, in which the parameters corresponding to θ and σ appearing in the Vasiček model are chosen to be deterministic functions of time,

$$dr(t) = (\theta(t) - \alpha r(t))dt + \sigma(t)dW(t), \tag{3.8}$$

where α is constant and $W(t)$ is a Brownian motion under the risk-neutral measure Q.

Integrating (3.8) from t to $s \geq t$, we have

$$r(s) = r(t)e^{-\alpha(s-t)} + \int_t^s \theta(u)e^{-\alpha(s-u)}du + \int_t^s \sigma(u)e^{-\alpha(s-u)}dW(u). \tag{3.9}$$

Adopting an approach analogous to that in the Vasiček model, we can derive an analytic expression for the zero-coupon bond price using the risk-neutral pricing formula (3.3). This yields

$$B(t,T) = \exp\left(-r(t)D(t,T) - \int_t^T \theta(u)D(u,T)du \right.$$

$$\left. + \frac{1}{2}\int_t^T \sigma(u)^2 D(u,T)^2 du \right), \tag{3.10}$$

where $D(t,T)$ is given by (3.5).

Exercise 3.4 Verify (3.10) for the Hull–White model by following a similar argument to that leading to formula (3.6) for the zero-coupon bond price in the Vasiček model.

The time-dependent parameter $\theta(t)$ can be chosen to match the current term structure. In fact, from (3.10) it can be seen that what is really needed is an expression for the integral $\int_t^T \theta(u)D(u,T)du$ rather than $\theta(t)$ itself. To this end we take

$$\ln \frac{B(0,T)}{B(0,t)} = -r(0)(D(0,T) - D(0,t)) - \int_t^T \theta(u)D(u,T)du$$

$$- \int_0^t \theta(u)\left(D(u,T) - D(u,t)\right)du + \frac{1}{2}\int_t^T \sigma(u)^2 D(u,T)^2 du$$

$$+ \frac{1}{2}\int_0^t \sigma(u)^2 \left(D(u,T)^2 - D(u,t)^2\right)du.$$

The integrals from 0 to t can be rewritten by using the relation

$$D(u,T) = D(u,t) + D_t(u,t)D(t,T), \tag{3.11}$$

where $D_t(u, t)$ is the partial derivative of $D(u, t)$ with respect to t, to yield

$$\ln \frac{B(0, T)}{B(0, t)} = -r(0)D_t(0, t)D(t, T) - \int_t^T \theta(u)D(u, T)du$$

$$- D(t, T) \int_0^t \theta(u)D_t(u, t)du + \frac{1}{2} \int_t^T \sigma(u)^2 D(u, T)^2 du$$

$$+ D(t, T) \int_0^t \sigma(u)^2 D(u, t)D_t(u, t)du + \frac{1}{2}D(t, T)^2 \int_0^t \sigma(u)^2 D_t(u, t)^2 du.$$

From (3.10), using formula (1.9) for the instantaneous forward rate, we obtain

$$f(0, t) = r(0)D_t(0, t) + \int_0^t \theta(u)D_t(u, t)du$$

$$- \int_0^t \sigma^2(u)D(u, t)D_t(u, t)du. \qquad (3.12)$$

It follows that

$$\ln \frac{B(0, T)}{B(0, t)} = -f(0, t)D(t, T) - \int_t^T \theta(u)D(u, T)du$$

$$+ \frac{1}{2} \int_t^T \sigma(u)^2 D(u, T)^2 du + \frac{1}{2}D(t, T)^2 \int_0^t \sigma(u)^2 D_t(u, t)^2 du,$$

which gives the desired expression for $\int_t^T \theta(u)D(u, T)du$ in terms of $B(0, t)$, $B(0, T)$ and $f(0, t)$, that is, in terms of the current term structure. Substituting this expression into (3.10), we get the following result.

Proposition 3.5
In the Hull–White model the zero-coupon bond price at time $t \geq 0$ that gives an exact fit to the term structure of interest rates at time 0 is

$$B(t, T) = \frac{B(0, T)}{B(0, t)} \exp\left(- (r(t) - f(0, t))D(t, T) \right.$$

$$\left. - \frac{1}{2}D(t, T)^2 \int_0^t \sigma(u)^2 D_t(u, t)^2 du \right), \quad (3.13)$$

where $D(t, T)$ is given by (3.5).

In addition to the bond price, it is also convenient to have the Hull–White short-rate process that gives an exact fit to the term structure at time 0.

From (3.12) we can see that

$$f(0, s) - e^{-\alpha(s-t)}f(0, t) = \int_t^s \theta(u)e^{-\alpha(s-u)}du - \int_0^s \sigma(u)^2 D(u, s)e^{-\alpha(s-u)}du$$
$$+ \int_0^t \sigma(u)^2 D(u, t)e^{-\alpha(s-u)}du.$$

Therefore (3.9) becomes

$$r(s) = (r(t) - f(0, t))\,e^{-\alpha(s-t)} + f(0, s) + \int_0^s \sigma(u)^2 D(u, s)e^{-\alpha(s-u)}du$$
$$- \int_0^t \sigma(u)^2 D(u, t)e^{-\alpha(s-u)}du + \int_t^s \sigma(u)e^{-\alpha(s-u)}dW(u). \quad (3.14)$$

Using the above expression in the pricing formula (3.3) for zero-coupon bonds provides another way of deriving (3.13).

Exercise 3.5   Derive the zero-coupon bond price (3.13) in the Hull–White model by using the Hull–White short-rate process (3.14).
   Hint: To simplify the calculations use the formulae

$$\int_t^T e^{-\alpha(s-t)}ds = D(t, T), \quad \int_t^T D(t, s)e^{-\alpha(s-t)}ds = \frac{1}{2}D(t, T)^2, \quad (3.15)$$

where $D(t, T)$ is given by (3.5).

Bond option formula

Consider a call and a put option with strike K and expiry S written on a zero-coupon bond with maturity $T > S$. From Theorem 2.4 and Exercise 2.9 we know that if the zero-coupon bond obeys (2.8) with deterministic log-volatility, then the prices at time 0 of the call and the put are

$$\mathbf{BC}(0; S, T, K) = B(0, T)N(d_+) - KB(0, S)N(d_-), \quad (3.16)$$
$$\mathbf{BP}(0; S, T, K) = KB(0, S)N(-d_-) - B(0, T)N(-d_+), \quad (3.17)$$

where

$$d_+ = \frac{\ln\frac{B(0,T)}{B(0,S)K} + \frac{1}{2}v(0, S)}{\sqrt{v(0, S)}}, \quad d_- = d_+ - v(0, S), \quad (3.18)$$

and $v(0, S)$ is the variance of $\ln B(S, T)$.

In the Hull–White model the zero-coupon bond price $B(S, T)$ is given by (3.10) with S substituted for t. The variance of $\ln B(S,T)$ is therefore equal to the variance of $-r(S)D(S,T)$, where $r(S)$ is given by (3.9) with S substituted for s and 0 for t. As a result,

$$v(0,S) = \text{Var}\left(D(S,T)\int_0^S \sigma(u)e^{-\alpha(S-u)}dW(u)\right)$$

$$= D(S,T)^2 \int_0^S \sigma(u)^2 e^{-2\alpha(S-u)}du. \tag{3.19}$$

This gives an analytic formula for the bond option price. When the time-dependent volatility term $\sigma(t)$ is chosen to be constant, (3.19) becomes

$$v(0,S) = \frac{\sigma^2}{2\alpha^3}\left(1 - e^{-\alpha(T-S)}\right)^2\left(1 - e^{-2\alpha S}\right). \tag{3.20}$$

Exercise 3.6   Derive formulae for calls and puts on a zero-coupon bond in the Merton model.

Exercise 3.7   Derive formulae for calls and puts on a zero-coupon bond in the Vasiček model. Compare these formulae with those for the Hull–White model with $\sigma(t)$ chosen to be constant. They should be identical. Why?

Formula for caps and floors

Consider a caplet with strike K, unit notional $N = 1$ and expiry T_i written on the spot LIBOR rate $L(T_{i-1}, T_i)$. In Section 2.7 we saw how the caplet payoff can be expressed as $1 + \tau_i K$ put options with strike $(1 + \tau_i K)^{-1}$ and expiry T_{i-1} written on a zero-coupon bond with maturity T_i. The price at time 0 of the caplet in the Hull–White model is

$$\mathbf{Cpl}_i(0) = (1 + \tau_i K)\mathbf{BP}\left(0; T_{i-1}, T_i, \frac{1}{1 + \tau_i K}\right), \tag{3.21}$$

where **BP** is the price of a put option on a zero-coupon bond given by (3.17) and (3.18), with the variance of $\ln B(S,T)$ given by (3.19). Similarly, the price of the corresponding floorlet is

$$\mathbf{Flr}_i(0) = (1 + \tau_i K)\mathbf{BC}\left(0; T_{i-1}, T_i, \frac{1}{1 + \tau_i K}\right), \qquad (3.22)$$

where $\mathbf{BC}$ is given by (3.16) and (3.18), with the variance of $\ln B(S, T)$ given by (3.19). The price of a cap (or floor) is simply the sum of the prices of the constituent caplets (or floorlets).

In general, the prices of caplets and floorlets are derived (via bootstrapping) from the market prices of caps and floors. Formulae (3.21) and (3.22) are used in calibrating the Hull–White model, where we use the known market prices to help us derive the model parameters.

Formula for swaptions

Consider an option with strike K and expiry T_0 on a payer interest rate swap with unit notional, settlement dates $T_1, \ldots, T_n$ and reset dates $T_0, \ldots, T_{n-1}$. In Section 2.8 we saw how the swaption payoff can be written as a put option with strike 1 on a coupon-bearing bond with coupon rate K, that is,

$$\left(1 - K \sum_{i=1}^{n} \tau_i B(T_0, T_i) - B(T_0, T_n)\right)^+. \qquad (3.23)$$

A method referred to as **Jamshidian's trick** can be applied to write this option on a coupon-bearing bond as a linear combination of put options on zero-coupon bonds. According to (3.10), the zero-coupon bond price $B(t, T) = F(t, r(t); T)$ in the Hull–White model is a decreasing function of the short rate $r(t)$. It follows that the coupon-bearing bond price $K \sum_{i=1}^{n} \tau_i F(t, r(t); T_i) + F(t, r(t); T_n)$ is also a decreasing function of $r(t)$, and there exists a critical value $\tilde{r}$ of the short rate such that

$$K \sum_{i=1}^{n} \tau_i F(T_0, \tilde{r}; T_i) + F(T_0, \tilde{r}; T_n) = 1. \qquad (3.24)$$

Letting $K_i = F(T_0, \tilde{r}; T_i)$ for $i = 1, \ldots, n$, so $K \sum_{i=1}^{n} \tau_i K_i + K_n = 1$, and observing that $B(T_0, T_i) < K_i$ if and only if $r(T_0) > \tilde{r}$, we can write the payoff (3.23) as

$$K \sum_{i=1}^{n} \tau_i (K_i - B(T_0, T_i))^+ + (K_n - B(T_0, T_n))^+.$$

Therefore the option on a coupon-bearing bond is a linear combination of options on the underlying zero-coupon bonds.

As a result, the price at time 0 of the swaption in the Hull–White model is given by

$$\text{PSwpt}_{0,n}(0) = \sum_{i=1}^{n} K(T_i - T_{i-1})\text{BP}(0; T_0, T_i, K_i) + \text{BP}(0; T_0, T_n, K_n), \quad (3.25)$$

where **BP** is given by (3.17) and (3.18), with the variance of $\ln B(S, T)$ given by (3.19).

Exercise 3.8 Suppose we have specified the value of α and the functional form of the volatility $\sigma(t)$. Explain how to estimate K_i for $i = 1, \ldots, n$ in the Hull–White swaption formula (3.25).

Calibrating the Hull–White model

The prices of the most liquid caps, floors and swaptions are given by the market. Therefore the left-hand sides of formulae (3.21), (3.22) and (3.25) are known. We can use these formulae to estimate the Hull–White model parameters given the market prices. Once we know the model parameters, we can then price complex or non-vanilla instruments. A common example of a non-vanilla instrument is the Bermudan swaption, which we will discuss in Section 3.6.

In Section 2.9 we introduced the notion of the implied Black caplet volatility (or spot volatility), which is the volatility parameter that must be inserted into the Black formula to obtain the market price of the caplet. Recall that, for the caplet maturing at time T_{i-1} and paying at time T_i, we denote the implied caplet volatility by $\hat{\sigma}_i^{\text{caplet}}$.

Formula (3.21) can be used to compute the volatility σ_i^{caplet} of the ith caplet implied by the Hull–White model. To this end we solve the equation

$$\text{Cpl}_i(0) = \text{Cpl}_i^{\text{Black}}(0; \sigma_i^{\text{caplet}}) \qquad (3.26)$$

with $\text{Cpl}_i(0)$ given by (3.21) and $\text{Cpl}_i^{\text{Black}}(0; \sigma_i^{\text{caplet}})$ by Black's formula (2.24).

The volatility term structure for the Hull–White model is given by solving equation (3.26) for each caplet. The model parameters are chosen so that the implied volatility σ_i^{caplet} of the ith caplet in the Hull–White model computed via (3.26) matches as best as possible the caplet spot volatility $\hat{\sigma}_i^{\text{caplet}}$ given by the market.

Similarly, we can calibrate to vanilla swaptions by choosing the model parameters so that the volatility implied by the swaption formula in the Hull–White model is as close as possible to the Black swaption volatility $\hat{\sigma}_{0,n}^{\text{swpt}}$ given by the market.

As a first attempt at calibration to the caplet or swaption market we could choose $\sigma(t)$ to be constant. However, in such cases we will generally not have enough degrees of freedom for an accurate fit. Therefore the typical assumption is that $\sigma(t)$ is piecewise constant. We partition the time axis by a sequence of dates $T_0 < T_1 < \cdots < T_n < T$ so that

$$\sigma(t) = \sigma_i \quad \text{for} \quad T_{i-1} < t \le T_i, \quad i = 1, \ldots, n, \tag{3.27}$$

and then choose a set of vanilla options to calibrate to. According to Proposition 3.5, the T-bond price at time T_i that gives an exact fit to the market term structure of interest rates at time 0 is

$$B(T_i, T) = \frac{B^{\text{mkt}}(0, T)}{B^{\text{mkt}}(0, T_i)} \exp\left(-(r(T_i) - f^{\text{mkt}}(0, T_i))D(T_i, T) \right.$$
$$\left. - \frac{1}{2}D^2(T_i, T) \sum_{k=1}^{i} \frac{\sigma_k}{2\alpha} \left(e^{-2\alpha(T_i - T_k)} - e^{-2\alpha(T_i - T_{k-1})} \right) \right),$$

where $D(T_i, T)$ is given by (3.5). The bond price depends only on the short-rate volatilities $\sigma_1, \ldots, \sigma_i$ and the mean-reversion term α.

Remark 3.6

Given the range of caps, floors and swaptions that are actively traded in the market, a natural question to ask is what subset of these do we actually use to calibrate our model? The standard market practice is to calibrate to what traders refer to as the 'natural hedging instruments'. These are the vanilla options used to hedge risk in the exotic instrument we are attempting to model. For the case of a Bermudan swaption, which we will discuss in Section 3.6, the risk is hedged by the underlying co-terminal swaptions.

Remark 3.7

For a given expiry T_i the Black implied volatility for strike K is read from a 'volatility cube' as described in Remark 2.10. The Hull–White short-rate model in itself does not account for the fact that the implied volatility for a given maturity varies with strike. However, correctly calibrated it will reproduce the correct market price of the underlying swaptions.

3.6 Bermudan swaptions in the Hull–White model

In this section we will use the formulae derived for the Hull–White model to price a non-vanilla instrument. The example we choose is a Bermudan swaption as defined in what follows.

The Hull–White short-rate process that gives an exact fit to the term-structure at time 0 is given by (3.14) under the risk-neutral measure Q. However, when we use the Hull–White model to price an exotic instrument or structured product, it can be convenient to know the drift of the short-rate process under the forward measure to calculate the option price. Therefore, we derive the dynamics of the short-rate process under the forward measure as a first step.

Hull–White under the forward measure

In Section 2.6 we saw in the case when the zero-coupon bond numeraire $B(t, T)$ obeys (2.8) that

$$W^T(t) = W(t) - \int_0^t \Sigma(u, T) du \quad \text{for all } t \in [0, T],$$

where $W(t)$ and $W^T(t)$ are Brownian motions under the risk-neutral measure Q and the forward measure P_T, respectively.

Applying the Itô formula to the bond price (3.10) and then using the above relationship between $W^T(t)$ and $W(t)$, we can show that the Hull–White SDE (3.8) for the short rate becomes

$$dr(t) = (\theta(t) - \alpha r(t) - \sigma(t)^2 D(t, T)) dt + \sigma(t) dW^T(t) \qquad (3.28)$$

under the forward measure.

> **Exercise 3.9** Show that (3.28) holds true.

Furthermore, using (3.14) we can write an expression for the Hull–White short rate at time $T > t$ that gives an exact fit to the term structure at time 0. Applying the same change of measure and then simplifying, we can see that $r(T)$ is given by

$$r(T) = (r(t) - f(0, t)) e^{-\alpha(T-t)} + f(0, T)$$
$$+ \int_0^t \sigma(u)^2 \frac{e^{-\alpha(T+t-2u)} - e^{-2\alpha(T-u)}}{\alpha} du + \int_t^T \sigma(u) e^{-\alpha(T-u)} dW^T(u)$$

$$(3.29)$$

under the forward measure P_T. This expression forms the basis of the numerical example we outline below. Note how the expectation of $r(T)$ given $r(t)$ depends only on $\sigma(u)$ for $u \in [0, t]$. Indeed, if we compare this to (3.14) (where we replace time s by T), we can see that working under the forward measure yields a simpler formula.

Bermudan swaption

Consider a unit notional amount and a set of dates $0 < T_0 < T_1 < \cdots < T_n$. The holder of a payer (or receiver) **Bermudan swaption** with strike K has the right to enter a payer (or receiver) interest rate swap at any time T_k for $k = 0, \ldots, l$ with $l < n$. The swap has reset dates $T_0, \ldots, T_n - 1$, settlement dates $T_1, \ldots, T_n$ and swap rate K. We assume that $l = n - 1$ and consider a payer Bermudan swaption, whose value at time 0 we denote by **Berm**(0). Note how this differs form the vanilla swaption, where the exercise date is fixed.

If the Bermudan swaption has not yet been exercised at time T_i for some $i < l$, then the holder has to decide whether to continue holding the option or to exercise immediately. The exercise value is

$$\mathrm{E}(T_i) = (\mathbf{PS}(T_i))^+.$$

Whether or not it is optimal to exercise at time T_i will depend on the value of holding the option until time T_{i+1}. We denote this value by $\mathrm{C}(T_i)$ and refer to it as the continuation value. The value of the swaption at time T_i is

$$\mathbf{Berm}(T_i) = \max(\mathrm{E}(T_i), \mathrm{C}(T_i)). \tag{3.30}$$

The continuation value at time T_i can be computed recursively. We have

$$\mathrm{C}(T_i) = B(T_i, T_{i+1})\mathbb{E}_{P_{T_{i+1}}}(\mathbf{Berm}(T_{i+1})|\,\mathcal{F}_{T_i}),$$

where the expectation is taken under the forward measure $P_{T_{i+1}}$.

Calibrating to co-terminal swaptions

As explained in Remark 3.6, we calibrate to the set of vanilla options used to hedge the exotic instrument. For the Bermudan swaption this is the underlying set of co-terminal swaptions. We minimise the difference between the Hull–White model price $\mathbf{PSwpt}_{i,n}(0)$ and the market price (as expressed by Black's swaption formula) $\mathbf{PSwpt}_{i,n}^{\mathrm{mkt}}(t) = \mathbf{PSwpt}_{i,n}^{\mathrm{Black}}(t; \hat{\sigma}_{i,n}^{\mathrm{swpt}})$ of the underlying set of swaptions for $i = 0, \ldots, n - 1$. More precisely, we solve the non-linear least squares optimisation problem

$$\min_{\sigma_1,\ldots,\sigma_n} \sum_{i=0}^{n-1}\left(\mathbf{PSwpt}_{i,n}(0) - \mathbf{PSwpt}_{i,n}^{\mathrm{mkt}}(0)\right)^2,$$

where $\mathbf{PSwpt}_{i,n}(0)$ depends on the short-rate volatility values $\sigma_1,\ldots,\sigma_n$. To ensure that the parameters are positive we generally perform a constrained optimisation, where we specify an upper and lower bound.

This calibrates the short-rate volatility values. For the mean-reversion parameter α we use the autocorrelation between the sort rates.

Mean-reversion parameter and autocorrelation

The mean-reversion parameter α controls the the correlation between the short rates at different points in time, i.e. the autocorrelation. For $s > t$ the autocorrelation is

$$\begin{aligned}\mathrm{Corr}(r(t), r(s)) &= \frac{\mathbb{E}(r(t)r(s))}{\sqrt{\mathrm{Var}(r(t))\mathrm{Var}(r(s))}} \\ &= \frac{\int_0^t \sigma^2(u)e^{-\alpha(t+s-2u)}du}{\sqrt{\int_0^t \sigma^2(u)e^{-2\alpha(t-u)}du \int_0^s \sigma^2(u)e^{-2\alpha(s-u)}du}}.\end{aligned}$$

If we assume that the volatility is constant, this can be simplified to

$$\mathrm{Corr}[r(t), r(s)] = \sqrt{\frac{e^{2\alpha t} - 1}{e^{2\alpha s} - 1}}.$$

Increasing the mean-reversion parameter α lowers the autocorrelation. This may have a significant impact on the valuation of exotic derivatives, and can be used to calibrate the value of α.

Numerical method

To apply the above recursive relation we begin by discretising the short rate domain, creating a grid of $N + 1$ values $r_0 < r_1 < \cdots < r_N$, where $r(0)$ is at a midpoint of the grid. Suppose that the time T_{i+1} Bermudan price $\mathbf{Berm}(T_{i+1}; r(T_{i+1}))$ is known for each grid point $r(T_{i+1}) = r_j$, and we want to compute $\mathbf{Berm}(T_i; r(T_i))$ at time T_i for each grid point $r(T_{i+1}) = r_j$. At time T_i the continuation value is

$$C(T_i; r(T_i)) = B(T_i, T_{i+1})\mathbb{E}_{P_{T_{i+1}}}(\mathbf{Berm}(T_{i+1}; r(T_{i+1}))|\mathscr{F}_{T_i}).$$

The zero-coupon bond price $B(T_i, T_{i+1})$ calibrated to the term structure at time 0 is given by (3.13), while the short rate calibrated to the term structure at time 0 is given by (3.29), namely

$$r(T_{i+1}) = (r(T_i) - f(0, T_i)) e^{-\alpha(T_{i+1}-T_i)} + f(0, T_{i+1})$$
$$+ \int_0^{T_i} \sigma(u)^2 \frac{e^{-\alpha(T_{i+1}+T_i-2u)} - e^{-2\alpha(T_{i+1}-u)}}{\alpha} du$$
$$+ \int_{T_i}^{T_{i+1}} \sigma(u) e^{-\alpha(T_{i+1}-u)} dW^{T_{i+1}}(u).$$

The stochastic integral in the last expression is independent of $\mathcal{F}_{T_i}$ and normally distributed with mean 0 and variance

$$s_i^2 = \int_{T_i}^{T_{i+1}} \sigma(u)^2 e^{-2\alpha(T_{i+1}-u)} du$$

under the forward measure $P_{T_{i+1}}$. Putting

$$m_i = (r(T_i) - f(0, T_i)) e^{-\alpha(T_{i+1}-T_i)} + f(0, T_{i+1})$$
$$+ \int_0^{T_i} \sigma(u)^2 \frac{e^{-\alpha(T_{i+1}+T_i-2u)} - e^{-2\alpha(T_{i+1}-u)}}{\alpha} du,$$

we therefore have

$$\mathbb{E}_{P_{T_{i+1}}}(\mathbf{Berm}(T_{i+1}; r(T_{i+1})) | \mathcal{F}_{T_i})$$
$$= \frac{1}{\sqrt{2\pi s_i^2}} \int_{-\infty}^{\infty} \mathbf{Berm}(T_{i+1}; x) \exp\left(-\frac{(x - m_i)^2}{2s_i^2}\right) dx.$$

The last integral can be evaluated numerically by using the known values of $\mathbf{Berm}(T_{i+1}; r(T_{i+1}))$ at the grid points $r(T_{i+1}) = r_j$. This makes it possible to compute the continuation value $C(T_i; r(T_i))$ and hence the Bermudan price $\mathbf{Berm}(T_i; r(T_i))$ from the recursive relation (3.30) at each grid point $r(T_i) = r_j$.

To evaluate the option we start at the last exercise date T_l and work backwards in time. At T_l the continuation value is zero as there is no benefit in holding the option beyond the last exercise date. Then we proceed backwards from T_i to T_{i-1} for $i = l, \ldots, 0$ using the above recursive relationships to arrive at the Bermudan prices $\mathbf{Berm}(0; r(0))$ at time 0 for all grid points $r(0) = r_j$.

3.7 Two-factor Hull–White model

Many vanilla options are only weakly affected by the correlation between rates of different maturities and can be adequately priced using a one-factor model. Even more complex options such as Bermudans can be handled using a one-factor model. However, many exotic options are particularly sensitive to how rates of different maturities are correlated and must be modelled in a multi-factor framework. These include options which depend in a non-linear way on the difference between two rates or options whose payoff depends on two different interest rate curves.

The model we are going to examine is a simple extension of the one-factor Hull–White model with a stochastic mean-reversion level added to the drift term. To assist in the derivation of analytic formulae this model is then reformulated as a Gaussian two-factor model. The calculations are slightly more involved than in the one-factor case, but the overall approach is similar.

The SDE (3.8) for the short rate in the Hull–White model can be modi-fied by adding a stochastic term $u(t)$ to the drift,

$$dr(t) = (\theta(t) + u(t) - \alpha r(t))dt + \delta dW(t), \qquad (3.31)$$

where α, δ are constants, $\theta(t)$ is a deterministic function of time and $W(t)$ is a Brownian motion under the risk-neutral measure Q. Moreover, $u(t)$ satisfies the SDE

$$du(t) = -\beta u(t)dt + \varepsilon dZ(t) \qquad (3.32)$$

with initial value $u(0) = 0$, where β and ε are constants and $Z(t)$ is another Brownian motion under the risk-neutral measure Q such that

$$dW(t)dZ(t) = \varrho dt \qquad (3.33)$$

for a constant ϱ, the correlation between the two Brownian motions. Addi-tionally, we assume that $\alpha \neq \beta$.

It is possible to obtain a bond pricing formula in terms of $r(t)$, $u(t)$ and the model parameters by following a similar argument to the derivation of formula (3.6) for the zero-coupon bond price in the Vasiček model and (3.10) in the one-factor Hull–White model. Though not difficult, this is rather involved. Instead, we represent the short rate in the two-factor Hull–White model as

$$r(t) = \phi(t) + x(t) + y(t), \qquad (3.34)$$

where $\phi(t)$ is a deterministic function and

$$dx(t) = -\alpha x(t)dt + \sigma dU(t), \qquad (3.35)$$

$$dy(t) = -\beta y(t)dt + \eta dV(t), \qquad (3.36)$$

with initial conditions $x(0) = 0$, $y(0) = 0$, and where α, β, σ and η are constants (in fact α, β are the same constants as in (3.31) and (3.32)), and $U(t)$ and $V(t)$ are Brownian motions under the risk-neutral measure Q such that

$$dU(t)dV(t) = \rho dt. \qquad (3.37)$$

Note that the correlation ρ between the Brownian motions $U(t)$ and $V(t)$ is not the same as the correlation ϱ between $W(t)$ and $Z(t)$.

Exercise 3.10 Show that in the two-factor Hull–White model defined by (3.31), (3.32) and (3.33) we can satisfy (3.34), (3.35), (3.36) and (3.37) if we set

$$\phi(t) = r(0)e^{-\alpha t} + \int_0^t \theta(s)e^{-\alpha(t-s)}ds,$$

$$y(t) = \frac{u(t)}{\alpha - \beta},$$

$$x(t) = r(t) - \phi(t) - y(t),$$

with constants σ, η and ρ, and Brownian motions $U(t)$ and $V(t)$ suitably defined in terms of $\alpha, \beta, \delta, \varepsilon, \varrho$ and $W(t), Z(t)$.

Gaussian two-factor approach

We have represented the two-factor Hull–White model (3.31), (3.32) as a **Gaussian two-factor model** (3.34), (3.35), (3.36), which helps us to derive a formula for zero-coupon bond prices.

Integrating (3.35) and (3.36) from t to s, we have

$$r(s) = \phi(s) + x(t)e^{-\alpha(s-t)} + y(t)e^{-\beta(s-t)}$$

$$+ \sigma \int_t^s e^{-\alpha(s-u)}dU(u) + \eta \int_t^s e^{-\beta(s-u)}dV(u). \qquad (3.38)$$

As was the case with the Vasiček and one-factor Hull–White models, we can derive an analytic expression for zero-coupon bonds using the pricing formula (3.3). Integrating the short rate and taking expectation yields

$$B(t,T) = \exp\left(- x(t)\frac{1 - e^{-\alpha(T-t)}}{\alpha} - y(t)\frac{1 - e^{-\beta(T-t)}}{\beta} \right.$$

$$\left. - \int_t^T \phi(s)ds + \frac{1}{2}V(t,T) \right), \tag{3.39}$$

where

$$V(t,T) = \frac{\sigma^2}{\alpha^2} \int_t^T \left(1 - e^{-\alpha(T-u)}\right)^2 du + \frac{\eta^2}{\beta^2} \int_t^T \left(1 - e^{-\beta(T-u)}\right)^2 du$$

$$+ 2\rho\frac{\sigma\eta}{\alpha\beta} \int_t^T \left(1 - e^{-\alpha(T-u)}\right)\left(1 - e^{-\beta(T-u)}\right)du. \tag{3.40}$$

Integrating, we get

$$V(t,T) = \frac{\sigma^2}{2\alpha^3} \left(-3 - e^{-2\alpha(T-t)} + 4e^{-\alpha(T-t)} + 2\alpha(T-t) \right)$$

$$+ \frac{\eta^2}{2\beta^3} \left(-3 - e^{-2\beta(T-t)} + 4e^{-\beta(T-t)} + 2\beta(T-t) \right)$$

$$+ 2\rho\frac{\sigma\eta}{\alpha\beta} \left(T - t - \frac{1 - e^{-\alpha(T-t)}}{\alpha} - \frac{1 - e^{-\beta(T-t)}}{\beta} + \frac{1 - e^{-(\alpha+\beta)(T-t)}}{\alpha+\beta} \right).$$

Exercise 3.11   Derive formula (3.39) for the bond price $B(t,T)$.

Fitting the current term structure

The time-dependent parameter $\phi(t)$ is chosen to fit the current interest rate term structure. If the model price fits the interest rate term structure at time 0 for any given maturity T, then we must have

$$B(0,T) = \exp\left(-\int_0^T \phi(s)ds + \frac{1}{2}V(0,T)\right).$$

Using (1.9), we find that the model fits the term structure at time 0 if

$$f(0,T) = \phi(T) - \frac{1}{2}\frac{\partial V(0,T)}{\partial T}, \tag{3.41}$$

where

$$\frac{\partial V(0,T)}{\partial T} = \frac{\sigma^2}{\alpha^2}\left(1 - e^{-\alpha T}\right)^2 + \frac{\eta^2}{\beta^2}\left(1 - e^{-\beta T}\right)^2 + 2\rho\frac{\sigma\eta}{\alpha\beta}\left(1 - e^{-\alpha T}\right)\left(1 - e^{-\beta T}\right).$$

Note that (3.41) gives us an expression for ϕ as a function of the instantaneous forward curve. However, we just need an expression for the integral of ϕ from time t to T rather than an explicit formula for ϕ. It is given by

$$\int_t^T \phi(s)ds = \ln \frac{B(0,t)}{B(0,T)} + \frac{1}{2}(V(0,T) - V(0,t)).$$

On substituting this into (3.39), we have following proposition.

Proposition 3.8
In the two-factor Hull–White model the zero-coupon bond price that gives an exact fit to the term structure of interest rates at time 0 is

$$B(t,T) = \frac{B(0,T)}{B(0,t)} \exp\left(-x(t)\frac{1-e^{-\alpha(T-t)}}{\alpha} - y(t)\frac{1-e^{-\beta(T-t)}}{\beta}\right.$$
$$\left. + \frac{1}{2}(V(0,t) - V(0,T) + V(t,T))\right), \qquad (3.42)$$

where V is given by (3.40) and $x(t), y(t)$ solve the SDEs (3.35), (3.36) with $x(0) = 0$ and $y(0) = 0$.

Bond option

In the two-dimensional Hull–White model the volatility of the logarithm of the bond price (3.42) is deterministic (see Exercise 3.12) and therefore the model yields an analytic formula for the bond option. The price at time 0 of a call option with strike K and expiry S written on a zero-coupon bond with maturity $T > S$ is given by

$$\mathbf{BC}(0; S, T, K) = B(0,T)N(d_+) - KB(0,S)N(d_-),$$

where

$$d_+ = \frac{\ln \frac{B(0,S)K}{B(0,T)} + \frac{1}{2}v(0,S)}{\sqrt{v(0,S)}}, \qquad d_- = d_+ - v(0,S)$$

with

$$v(0,S) = \frac{\sigma^2}{2\alpha^3}\left(1-e^{-\alpha(T-S)}\right)^2\left(1-e^{-2\alpha S}\right) + \frac{\eta^2}{2\beta^3}\left(1-e^{-\beta(T-S)}\right)^2\left(1-e^{-2\beta S}\right)$$
$$+ \frac{2\rho\sigma\eta}{\alpha\beta(\alpha+\beta)}\left(1 - e^{-\alpha(T-S)}\right)\left(1 - e^{-\beta(T-S)}\right)\left(1 - e^{-(\alpha+\beta)S}\right). \quad (3.43)$$

Exercise 3.12   Show that the variance of $\ln B(S, T)$ is given by (3.43).

Caps and floors

Since both caps and floors can be expressed in terms of bond options, it is possible to derive an analytic expression for these instruments within the two-factor Hull–White model. The approach is identical to that in the one-factor case, so is not reproduced here. The key ingredient for these formulae is the log-variance of the bond price given by the formula above.

4

Models of the forward rate

Heath–Jarrow–Morton (HJM) models are driven by the evolution in time t of the instantaneous forward-rate curve $f(t, T)$ parameterised by the maturity date T. The entire curve serves as the state variable. This is in contrast to short-rate models, which are driven by the evolution of a single point on the curve, the short rate $r(t)$.

Just like in the case of short-rate models, we adopt Assumption 2.1, i.e. we assume the existence of a risk-neutral measure Q, which transforms all security prices discounted by the money market account into martingales.

The key result in this framework is that the drift of the forward rate $f(t, T)$ under the risk-neutral measure Q is determined by the volatility. This is different to short-rate models, where we are free to specify the drift for the short rate. Compare this to the classical Black–Scholes model, where the drift of the underlying stock price process under the risk-neutral measure is equal to the spot interest rate; see [BSM]. In the HJM framework, just like in the Black–Scholes model, the drift of the underlying process (the instantaneous forward rate and the stock price, respectively) is fixed.

The main benefit of HJM models is that they allow for a perfect fit to the initial interest rate term structure and offer more flexibility than short-rate models. However, they can be difficult to apply in practice.

4.1 One-factor HJM models

Heath, Jarrow and Morton proposed a framework for modelling stochastic interest rates based on the dynamics of the instantaneous forward rate $f(t, T)$. We begin with the general assumption that the forward rate is an Itô process such that, for each maturity $T > 0$,

$$df(t, T) = \alpha(t, T)dt + \sigma(t, T)dW(t) \qquad (4.1)$$

for $t \in [0, T]$, where $W(t)$ is a Brownian motion under the risk-neutral measure Q. The stochastic differential $df(t, T)$ is applied to the t variable, whereas T is treated as a parameter. We have infinitely many processes $f(t, T)$ parameterised by T, each driven by the same Brownian motion $W(t)$.

Next we present a heuristic argument to establish a relationship between the drift $\alpha(t, T)$ and volatility $\sigma(t, T)$ of the forward-rate process and obtain an SDE for the zero-coupon bond price $B(t, T)$. By (1.11), the bond price can be expressed in terms of forward rates as

$$B(t, T) = \exp\left(-\int_t^T f(t, u)du\right).$$

To apply the Itô formula to the exponent on the right-hand side we need to compute the stochastic differential of $\int_t^T f(t, u)du$ with respect to the t variable, which appears in two places, in the lower integration limit and as an argument of $f(t, u)$. An informal calculation gives

$$d\left(\int_t^T f(t, u)du\right)$$

$$= -f(t, t)dt + \int_t^T \left(\alpha(t, u)dt + \sigma(t, u)dW(t)\right)du$$

$$= -r(t)dt + \left(\int_t^T \alpha(t, u)du\right)dt + \left(\int_t^T \sigma(t, u)du\right)dW(t). \qquad (4.2)$$

The term $f(t, t)dt = r(t)dt$ comes from differentiating with respect to the lower integration limit t, while the remaining terms come from using (4.1) to write the stochastic differential $df(t, u)$ with respect to t as $\alpha(t, u)dt + \sigma(t, u)dW(t)$ and moving dt and $dW(t)$ outside the integral. We have no guarantee that these transformations are legitimate, though they appear natural. A precise argument requires more work and some technical assumptions. This will be done below.

Now that we have the above expression for $d\left(\int_t^T f(t, u)du\right)$, it is a matter of using the Itô formula to obtain

$$dB(t, T) = \left(r(t) - \int_t^T \alpha(t, u)du + \frac{1}{2} \left(\int_t^T \sigma(t, u)du \right)^2 \right) B(t, T)dt$$
$$- \left(\int_t^T \sigma(t, u)du \right) B(t, T)dW(t).$$

From Exercise 2.3 we know that

$$r(t) - \int_t^T \alpha(t, u)du + \frac{1}{2} \left(\int_t^T \sigma(t, u)du \right)^2 = r(t),$$

which means that

$$\int_t^T \alpha(t, u)du = \frac{1}{2} \left(\int_t^T \sigma(t, u)du \right)^2.$$

Differentiating both sides with respect to T gives

$$\alpha(t, T) = \sigma(t, T) \int_t^T \sigma(t, u)du.$$

We are ready to summarise these results as a theorem. The technical assumptions concerning α and σ in this theorem allow us to swap the order of integration for ordinary and stochastic iterated integrals, which lends legitimacy to the above informal argument where we move dt and $dW(t)$ outside the integral with respect to du.

Theorem 4.1

Suppose that the forward rates $f(t, T)$ satisfy (4.1), that is,

$$df(t, T) = \alpha(t, T)dt + \sigma(t, T)dW(t),$$

where $W(t)$ is a Brownian motion under the risk-neutral measure Q, and where we assume that $\sigma(t, T)$ is adapted to the filtration $\mathcal{F}_t$ for each $T > 0$, and

$$\int_0^T \int_0^T |\alpha(s, u)| \, ds \, du < \infty, \qquad \int_0^T \left(\int_0^T |\sigma(s, u)|^2 \, ds \right)^{1/2} du < \infty$$

almost surely. Then

$$\alpha(t, T) = \sigma(t, T) \int_t^T \sigma(t, u)du. \qquad (4.3)$$

Therefore the dynamics of $f(t, T)$ under the risk-neutral measure Q is

$$f(t, T) = f(0, T) + \int_0^t \sigma(s, T) \left(\int_s^T \sigma(s, u)du \right) ds + \int_0^t \sigma(s, T)dW(s).$$

Furthermore the zero-coupon bond prices satisfy the SDE

$$dB(t, T) = r(t)B(t, T)dt + \Sigma(t, T)B(t, T)dW(t) \qquad (4.4)$$

with log-volatility

$$\Sigma(t, T) = -\int_t^T \sigma(t, u)du.$$

Proof A rigorous proof of (4.2) is all that remains to be done. We write (4.1) in integral form as

$$f(t, T) = f(0, T) + \int_0^t \alpha(s, T)ds + \int_0^t \sigma(s, T)dW(s). \qquad (4.5)$$

It follows that

$$r(t) = f(t, t) = f(0, t) + \int_0^t \alpha(s, t)ds + \int_0^t \sigma(s, t)dW(s).$$

Integrating, we get

$$\int_t^T f(t, u)du$$

$$= \int_t^T f(0, u)du + \int_t^T \left(\int_0^t \alpha(s, u)ds \right) du + \int_t^T \left(\int_0^t \sigma(s, u)dW(s) \right) du$$

and

$$\int_0^t r(u)du$$

$$= \int_0^t f(0, u)du + \int_0^t \left(\int_0^u \alpha(s, u)ds \right) du + \int_0^t \left(\int_0^u \sigma(s, u)dW(s) \right) du.$$

The assumptions on α and σ allow us to apply the Fubini theorem (see [PF]) to swap the iterated integrals with respect to ds and du, and the stochastic Fubini theorem[1] to swap the integrals with respect to $dW(s)$ and du,

$$\int_t^T f(t, u)du$$

$$= \int_t^T f(0, u)du + \int_0^t \left(\int_t^T \alpha(s, u)du \right) ds + \int_0^t \left(\int_t^T \sigma(s, u)du \right) dW(s)$$

---

[1] See M. Veraar, The stochastic Fubini theorem revisited, *Stochastics 84*, (2012), 543–551.

and

$$\int_0^t r(u)du$$

$$= \int_0^t f(0,u)du + \int_0^t \left(\int_s^t \alpha(s,u)du \right) ds + \int_0^t \left(\int_s^t \sigma(s,u)du \right) dW(s).$$

Hence

$$\int_t^T f(t,u)du$$

$$= \int_0^T f(0,u)du + \int_0^t \left(\int_s^T \alpha(s,u)du \right) ds + \int_0^t \left(\int_s^T \sigma(s,u)du \right) dW(s)$$

$$- \int_0^t f(0,u)du - \int_0^t \left(\int_s^t \alpha(s,u)du \right) ds - \int_0^t \left(\int_s^t \sigma(s,u)du \right) dW(s)$$

$$= \int_0^T f(0,u)du + \int_0^t \left(\int_s^T \alpha(s,u)du \right) ds + \int_0^t \left(\int_s^T \sigma(s,u)du \right) dW(s)$$

$$- \int_0^t r(u)du.$$

This proves (4.2). □

4.2 Gaussian models

Models with deterministic forward-rate volatility $\sigma(t,T)$ are referred to as **Gaussian models**. Their advantage is that it is possible to derive analytic formulae for calls and puts on a zero-coupon bond. When $\sigma(t,T)$ is deterministic, then both the forward rate and the short rate are normally distributed and the zero-coupon bond price is log-normally distributed under the risk-neutral measure Q. This leads to the familiar Black–Scholes type formulae for bond options.

Example 4.2
As a simple example, we take constant $\sigma(t,T)$, that is, $\sigma(t,T) = \sigma$ for all $t \leq T$. By Theorem 4.1, we must have

$$\alpha(t,T) = \sigma \int_t^T \sigma du = \sigma^2(T-t)$$

and

$$f(t,T) = f(0,T) + \int_0^t \alpha(s,T)ds + \int_0^t \sigma(s,T)dW(s)$$

$$= f(0,T) + \frac{1}{2}\sigma^2 t(2T - t) + \sigma W(t).$$

It follows that the short rate

$$r(t) = f(t,t) = f(0,t) + \frac{1}{2}\sigma^2 t^2 + \sigma W(t)$$

satisfies the SDE of the Ho–Lee model (see Table 3.1)

$$dr(t) = \theta(t)dt + \sigma dW(t)$$

with

$$\theta(t) = \frac{\partial f(0,t)}{\partial t} + \sigma^2 t.$$

Exercise 4.1   In the Ho–Lee model, i.e. when $\sigma(t,T) = \sigma$ is constant, show that

$$B(t,T) = \exp\left(-(T-t)(r(t) - f(0,t)) - \int_t^T f(0,s)ds - \frac{1}{2}\sigma^2 t(T-t)^2\right).$$

Example 4.3

Take $\sigma(t,T) = \sigma(t)e^{-\alpha(T-t)}$, where $\sigma(t)$ is a deterministic function and α is a constant. By Theorem 4.1, we have

$$\alpha(t,T) = \sigma(t,T) \int_t^T \sigma(t,u)du$$

$$= \sigma(t)^2 e^{-\alpha(T-t)} \int_t^T e^{-\alpha(T-u)}du = \sigma(t)^2 e^{-\alpha(T-t)} D(t,T),$$

where $D(t,T)$ is given by (3.5). As a result,

$$f(t,T) = f(0,T) + \int_0^t \alpha(s,T)ds + \int_0^t \sigma(s,T)dW(s)$$

$$= f(0,T) + \int_0^t \sigma(s)^2 e^{-\alpha(T-s)} D(s,T)ds + \int_0^t \sigma(s)e^{-\alpha(T-s)}dW(s)$$

and

$$r(t) = f(t,t) = f(0,t) + \int_0^t \sigma(s)^2 e^{-\alpha(t-s)} D(s,t) ds + \int_0^t \sigma(s) e^{-\alpha(t-s)} dW(s).$$

The short rate satisfies the SDE of the Hull–White model

$$dr(t) = (\theta(t) - \alpha r(t)) dt + \sigma(t) dW(t)$$

with

$$\theta(t) = \frac{\partial f(0,t)}{\partial t} + \alpha f(0,t) + \int_0^t \sigma(s)^2 e^{-2\alpha(t-s)} ds.$$

Gaussian HJM with separable volatility

For a general $\sigma(t,T)$ the drift term of the forward rate (and the short rate) is rather complicated. To simplify $\sigma(t,T)$ is often expressed as

$$\sigma(t,T) = \xi(t)\eta(T), \tag{4.6}$$

where $\xi(t)$ and $\eta(T)$ are strictly positive deterministic functions. With this choice of so-called **separable volatility**, the forward rate $f(t,T)$ is given by

$$f(t,T) = f(0,T) + \int_0^t \xi(s)\eta(T) \left(\int_s^T \xi(s)\eta(u) du \right) ds + \int_0^t \xi(s)\eta(T) dW(s),$$

and the short rate $r(t)$ is

$$r(t) = f(0,t) + \int_0^t \xi(s)\eta(t) \left(\int_s^t \xi(s)\eta(u) du \right) ds + \int_0^t \xi(s)\eta(t) dW(s).$$

Using the above, we can replace the stochastic integral in the expression for $f(t,T)$ to get

$$f(t,T) = f(0,T) + \frac{\eta(T)}{\eta(t)} (r(t) - f(0,t))$$

$$+ \int_0^t \xi(s)\eta(T) \left(\int_t^T \xi(s)\eta(u) du \right) ds. \tag{4.7}$$

We can see that the forward rate can be expressed in terms of the short rate. Moreover, by (1.11), we find that

$$B(t,T) = \exp\left(-\int_t^T f(0,u)du - \frac{r(t) - f(0,t)}{\eta(t)} \int_t^T \eta(u)du\right.$$
$$\left. - \int_t^T \int_0^t \xi(s)\eta(v)\left(\int_t^v \xi(s)\eta(u)du\right)dsdv\right).$$

We can simplify the above by changing the order of integration in the triple integral and calculating

$$\int_t^T \int_0^t \xi(s)\eta(v)\left(\int_t^v \xi(s)\eta(u)du\right)dsdv$$

$$= \int_0^t \int_t^T \xi(s)\eta(v)\left(\int_t^v \xi(s)\eta(u)du\right)dvds$$

$$= \int_0^t \xi(s)^2\left[\int_t^T \eta(v)\left(\int_t^v \eta(u)du\right)dv\right]ds.$$

The integral inside the square brackets can be simplified by noting that

$$\int_t^T \eta(v)\left(\int_t^v \eta(u)du\right)dv = \frac{1}{2}\left(\int_t^T \eta(u)du\right)^2.$$

Setting

$$I(t,T) = \frac{1}{\eta(t)}\int_t^T \eta(u)du,$$

we can write the zero-coupon bond price in a Gaussian HJM model with separable volatility as

$$B(t,T) = \exp\left(-\int_t^T f(0,u)du - (r(t) - f(0,t))I(t,T)\right.$$
$$\left. - \frac{1}{2}I(t,T)^2 \int_0^t \xi(s)^2\eta(t)^2 ds\right). \tag{4.8}$$

Exercise 4.2 In Example 4.3 we chose $\sigma(t,T) = \sigma(t)e^{-\alpha(T-t)}$, where $\sigma(t)$ is a deterministic function and α is a constant, and saw that the short-rate process satisfies the SDE of the Hull–White model. Using (4.8), show that the zero-coupon bond pricing formula is given by (3.13).

Example 4.4

An example of a Gaussian HJM model with separable volatility is the **Ritchken–Sankarasubramanian model**. Here the functions $\xi(t)$ and $\eta(t)$ take the form

$$\xi(t) = \sigma(t)\exp\left(\int_0^t \alpha(u)du\right), \quad \eta(t) = \exp\left(-\int_0^t \alpha(u)du\right),$$

where σ and α are deterministic functions.

For this choice of volatility the HJM model is equivalent to the general Hull–White model (i.e. the version where the mean-reversion parameter α is time dependent). This is often how the Hull–White model is implemented in practice.

Exercise 4.3 Show that in the Ritchken–Sankarasubramanian model the short rate satisfies the SDE

$$dr(t) = \left(\frac{\partial f(0,t)}{\partial t} + \phi(t) + \alpha(t)(f(0,t) - r(t))\right)dt + \sigma(t)dW(t),$$

where

$$\phi(t) = \int_0^t \sigma(s)^2 \exp\left(-2\int_s^t \alpha(u)du\right)ds.$$

Bond option price in Gaussian HJM model

In the HJM model the bond price satisfies the SDE (4.4),

$$dB(t,T) = r(t)B(t,T)dt + \Sigma(t,T)B(t,T)dW(t)$$

with log-volatility

$$\Sigma(t,T) = -\int_t^T \sigma(t,u)du.$$

For deterministic $\sigma(t,T)$ the log-volatility $\Sigma(t,T)$ is also deterministic. From Theorem 2.4 we know that the price at time t of a call option with strike K and expiry S written on a zero-coupon bond with maturity $T > S$ is

$$\mathbf{BC}(t; S, T, K) = B(t,T)N(d_+) - KB(t,S)N(d_-),$$

where

$$d_+ = \frac{\ln \frac{B(t,T)}{B(t,S)K} + \frac{1}{2}v(t,S)}{\sqrt{v(t,S)}}, \qquad d_- = d_+ - \sqrt{v(t,S)},$$

with

$$v(t,S) = \int_t^S \left(\Sigma(u,T) - \Sigma(u,S)\right)^2 du = \int_t^S \left(\int_S^T \sigma(u,v)dv\right)^2 du.$$

Mercurio–Moreleda model

Example 4.5

A financially plausible choice of volatility in a Gaussian HJM model is one that depends on the time to maturity. For example, the volatility of the forward rate can be taken as

$$\sigma(t,T) = \sigma(\gamma(T - t) + 1)e^{-\frac{\lambda}{2}(T-t)}, \tag{4.9}$$

where σ, γ and λ are positive constants such that $2\gamma > \lambda$. This is known as the **Mercurio–Moraleda model**.

Exercise 4.4 Show that $\sigma(t,T)$ in the Mercurio–Moraleda model is a hump-shaped function of T. Specifically, show that $\sigma(t,T)$ is increasing in T for $t \le T \le t + \frac{2\gamma-\lambda}{\gamma\lambda}$, has a maximum at $T = t + \frac{2\gamma-\lambda}{\gamma\lambda}$, and is decreasing in T for $t + \frac{2\gamma-\lambda}{\gamma\lambda} \le T$.

In the next exercise we compute the prices of calls and puts written on a zero-coupon bond in the Mercurio–Moraleda model in terms of the parameters σ, γ, λ.

Exercise 4.5 Show that the prices at time t of European calls and puts with maturity S and strike K written on a T-bond, where $t < S < T$, in the Mercurio–Moraleda model (4.9) are given by (2.21), (2.22),

(2.18) and (2.20) with

$$v(t, S) = \frac{4\sigma^2}{\lambda^4} \int_t^S (A - Bu)^2 \, e^{\lambda u} du$$

$$= \frac{4\sigma^2}{\lambda^5} B^2 \left(S^2 e^{\lambda S} - t^2 e^{\lambda t} \right) - \frac{8\sigma^2}{\lambda^6} B (B + A\lambda) \left(S e^{\lambda S} - t e^{\lambda t} \right)$$

$$+ \frac{4\sigma^2}{\lambda^7} \left(2B^2 + 2AB\lambda + A^2 \lambda^2 \right) \left(e^{\lambda S} - e^{\lambda t} \right),$$

where

$$A = (\gamma \lambda T + \lambda + 2\gamma) \, e^{-\frac{\lambda}{2} T} - (\gamma \lambda S + \lambda + 2\gamma) \, e^{-\frac{\lambda}{2} S},$$

$$B = \gamma \lambda \left(e^{-\frac{\lambda}{2} T} - e^{-\frac{\lambda}{2} S} \right).$$

4.3 Calibration

To obtain a working model within the HJM framework we can proceed as follows.

First we specify the functional form of the volatility $\sigma(t, T)$ of the forward rate, depending on some constant parameters. Functional forms where the volatility is a decreasing function of time to maturity are popular, such as the Hull–White forward-rate volatility in Example 4.3.

Once we have specified the functional form for $\sigma(t, T)$, the drift $\alpha(t, T)$ of the forward rate can be computed from (4.3). The initial term structure $f^{\text{mkt}}(0, T)$ of forward rates given by the market is then substituted for $f(0, T)$ in (4.5), so we get

$$f(t, T) = f^{\text{mkt}}(0, T) + \int_0^t \alpha(t, u) du + \int_0^t \sigma(t, u) dW(u).$$

Finally, the parameters in the functional form adopted for $\sigma(t, T)$ are chosen so that we match the market prices (or equivalently the implied volatilities) of a set of vanilla instruments such as caps or swaptions.

4.4 Multi-factor HJM models

In a one-factor model such as (4.1) the forward rates are driven by a one-dimensional Brownian motion. By contrast, in a multi-factor HJM model the forward-rate process is driven by n independent Brownian motions. For each maturity $T > 0$ the forward rate evolves as

$$df(t,T) = \alpha(t,T)dt + \sum_{i=1}^{n} \sigma_i(t,T)dW_i(t) \qquad (4.10)$$

for $t \in [0,T]$, where the volatility $\sigma(t,T) = (\sigma_1(t,T),\ldots,\sigma_n(t,T))$ is an n-dimensional vector-valued process, and $W(t) = (W_1(t),\ldots,W_n(t))$ is an n-dimensional Brownian motion under the risk-neutral measure Q.

The analysis in Section 4.1 can be applied to (4.10) to prove the following result.

Theorem 4.6
Suppose that the forward rates $f(t,T)$ satisfy (4.10) and assume that the volatilities $\sigma_1(t,T),\ldots,\sigma_n(t,T)$ are adapted to the filtration $\mathcal{F}_t$ for each $T > 0$, and

$$\int_0^T \int_0^T |\alpha(s,u)|\,ds\,du < \infty, \qquad \int_0^T \left(\int_0^T \sum_{i=1}^{n} |\sigma_i(s,u)|^2\,ds\right)^{1/2} du < \infty$$

almost surely. Then

$$\alpha(t,T) = \sum_{i=1}^{n} \sigma_i(t,T) \int_t^T \sigma_i(t,u)du. \qquad (4.11)$$

Therefore the dynamics of $f(t,T)$ under the risk-neutral measure Q is

$$f(t,T) = f(0,T) + \int_0^t \sum_{i=1}^{n} \sigma_i(s,T)\left(\int_s^T \sigma_i(s,u)du\right)ds$$

$$+ \int_0^t \sum_{i=1}^{n} \sigma_i(s,T)dW_i(s).$$

Furthermore, the zero-coupon bond prices satisfy the SDE

$$dB(t,T) = r(t)B(t,T)dt + \sum_{i=1}^{n} \Sigma_i(t,T)B(t,T)dW_i(t), \qquad (4.12)$$

with

$$\Sigma_i(t,T) = -\int_t^T \sigma_i(t,u)du$$

for $i = 1,\ldots,n$.

Two-factor Gaussian model

In the HJM two-factor framework the forward rate is given by

$$df(t, T) = \sum_{i=1}^{2} \left(\sigma_i(t, T) \int_t^T \sigma_i(t, u)du \right) dt + \sum_{i=1}^{2} \sigma_i(t, T)dW_i(t),$$

where $W_1(t)$, $W_2(t)$ are independent Brownian motions under the risk-neutral measure Q.

A popular choice for the volatilities is

$$\sigma_1(t, T) = \sigma_{11}e^{-\alpha_1(T-t)}, \quad \sigma_2(t, T) = \sigma_{21}e^{-\alpha_1(T-t)} + \sigma_{22}e^{-\alpha_2(T-t)}, \quad (4.13)$$

where $\sigma_{11}, \sigma_{21}, \sigma_{22}$ and α_1, α_2 are constants. For a suitable choice of constants this is the HJM equivalent of the Gaussian two-factor model (3.34), (3.35), (3.36), (3.37), or equivalently the two-factor Hull–White model in Section 3.7.

To see this we first express the correlated Brownian motions $U(t)$ and $V(t)$ in (3.35) and (3.36) as

$$U(t) = \sqrt{1 - \rho^2}W_1(t) + \rho W_2(t),$$
$$V(t) = W_2(t).$$

Therefore (3.35) and (3.36) become

$$dx(t) = -\alpha x(t)dt + \sigma(\sqrt{1 - \rho^2}dW_1(t) + \rho dW_2(t)),$$
$$dy(t) = -\beta y(t)dt + \eta dW_2(t).$$

By (3.42), for the two-factor Hull–White short-rate process the zero-coupon bond price at time $t \geq 0$ is

$$B(t, T) = \frac{B(0, T)}{B(0, t)} \exp\left(-x(t)\frac{1 - e^{-\alpha(T-t)}}{\alpha} - y(t)\frac{1 - e^{-\beta(T-t)}}{\beta} \right.$$
$$\left. + \frac{1}{2}(V(0, t) - V(0, T) + V(t, T)) \right),$$

where V is given by (3.40). Hence we have

$$dB(t, T) = B(t, T)r(t)dt + B(t, T)(\Sigma_1(t, T)dW_1(t) + \Sigma_2(t, T)W_2(t))$$

with

$$\Sigma_1(t, T) = -\int_t^T \sigma_1(t, u)du = -\sigma\sqrt{1 - \rho^2}\frac{1 - e^{-\alpha(T-t)}}{\alpha},$$
$$\Sigma_2(t, T) = -\int_t^T \sigma_2(t, u)du = -\sigma\rho\frac{1 - e^{-\alpha(T-t)}}{\alpha} - \eta\frac{1 - e^{-\beta(T-t)}}{\beta}.$$

Therefore

$$\sigma_1(t, T) = \sigma \sqrt{1 - \rho^2} e^{-\alpha(T-t)},$$
$$\sigma_2(t, T) = \sigma \rho e^{-\alpha(T-t)} + \eta e^{-\beta(T-t)}.$$

Comparing this with (4.13), we can see that $\sigma_{11} = \sigma \sqrt{1 - \rho^2}$, $\sigma_{21} = \sigma \rho$, $\sigma_{22} = \eta$ and $\alpha_1 = \alpha$, $\alpha_2 = \beta$.

4.5 Forward rate under the forward measure

The forward-rate dynamics under the risk-neutral measure Q is given by (4.10). We now derive the dynamics of $f(t, T)$ under the forward measure P_U for a settlement date $U \geq T$. Recall that this is the measure associated with $B(t, U)$ as numeraire.

From Section 2.2 we know that P_U is a probability measure equivalent to Q with Radon–Nikodym derivative

$$\frac{dP_U}{dQ} = \frac{1}{B(U)B(0, U)}.$$

Since $\frac{B(t,U)}{B(t)}$ is a martingale under Q, we have the density process

$$\xi(t) := \left. \frac{dP_U}{dQ} \right|_t = \mathbb{E}_Q \left(\frac{1}{B(U)B(0, U)} \middle| \mathcal{F}_t \right) = \frac{B(t, U)}{B(t)B(0, U)}$$

with $\xi(0) = 1$. The zero-coupon bond prices $B(t, U)$ satisfy SDE (4.12), hence $\xi(t)$ satisfies the SDE

$$\frac{d\xi(t)}{\xi(t)} = \sum_{i=1}^{n} \Sigma_i(t, U) dW_i(t),$$

with solution

$$\xi(t) = \exp\left(-\frac{1}{2} \int_0^t \sum_{i=1}^{n} \Sigma_i(s, U)^2 ds + \int_0^t \sum_{i=1}^{n} \Sigma_i(s, U) dW_i(s) \right),$$

where

$$\Sigma_i(t, U) = -\int_t^U \sigma_i(t, u) du \quad \text{for } i = 1, \ldots, n.$$

By the Girsanov theorem (see [BSM]), the process $(W_1^U(t), \ldots, W_n^U(t))$ with

$$W_i^U(t) = W_i(t) - \int_0^t \Sigma_i(s, U)ds$$

$$= W_i(t) + \int_0^t \left(\int_s^U \sigma_i(s, u)du \right) ds \quad \text{for } i = 1, \ldots, n$$

is an n-dimensional Brownian motion under P_U. Substitution of the above into (4.10) with $\alpha(t, T)$ given by (4.11) yields

$$df(t, T) = \sum_{i=1}^n \sigma_i(t, T) \left(\int_t^T \sigma_i(t, u)du \right) dt + \sum_{i=1}^n \sigma_i(t, T)dW_i(t)$$

$$= \sum_{i=1}^n \sigma_i(t, T) \left(\int_t^T \sigma_i(t, u)du \right) dt$$

$$+ \sum_{i=1}^n \sigma_i(t, T)dW_i^U(t) - \sum_{i=1}^n \sigma_i(t, T) \left(\int_t^U \sigma_i(t, u)du \right) dt$$

$$= -\sum_{i=1}^n \sigma_i(t, T) \left(\int_T^U \sigma_i(t, u)du \right) dt + \sum_{i=1}^n \sigma_i(t, T)dW_i^U(t). \quad (4.14)$$

Exercise 4.6 Suppose that $\mathbb{E}_{P_T} \left(\int_0^T \sum_{i=1}^n \sigma_i(t, T)^2 dt \right) < \infty$. Show that the forward rate $f(t, T)$ is a martingale under the forward measure P_T and, in particular,

$$f(t, T) = \mathbb{E}_{P_T} \left(r(T) | \mathcal{F}_t \right).$$

Exercise 4.7 From (4.14) we have that the short rate $r(T)$ is given by

$$r(T) = f(t, T) + \int_t^T \sum_{i=1}^n \sigma_i(s, T)dW_i^T(s). \quad (4.15)$$

For $\sigma(t, T) = \sigma(t)e^{-\alpha(T-t)}$, where $\sigma(t)$ is a deterministic function and α is a constant, derive (3.29), the Hull–White short-rate process under the forward measure P_T at time $T > t$ that gives an exact fit to the term structure at time 0.

5

LIBOR and swap market models

In the previous chapters we presented models based on the instantaneous short rate and the instantaneous forward rate. These models suffer from a number of drawbacks. Firstly, calibration to the prices of commonly traded vanilla instruments such as caps, floors or swaptions can be quite involved. Exotic derivatives depending on the volatilities of many different rates may need to be calibrated to a large set of market instruments, which is difficult when using a short-rate model. Secondly, although instantaneous rates are mathematically convenient, they are not directly observable in the market, nor are they related in a straightforward manner to the prices of any traded instruments. It can be difficult to relate the model parameters, such as mean-reversion in the Hull–White model, to a market-observable quantity.

In the LIBOR market model (LMM) we are going to use market rates, namely the forward LIBOR rates, as state variables modelled by a set of stochastic differential equations. For a suitable choice of numeraire we will express the drifts in these SDEs as functions of the volatilities and correlations among the forward rates.

A remarkable feature of the LMM is that the model prices are consistent with Black's formula. For a given forward LIBOR rate setting at time S and maturing at time $T > S$, the forward-rate dynamics is driftless under the forward measure P_T. This is consistent with Black's formula for caplets, where the LIBOR rate underlying each caplet is a log-normal process. Using these facts, we shall see how Black's formula arises naturally in the LMM framework. This is a major advantage of the LMM. It means that we can calibrate to implied (at-the-money) cap volatilities automatically.

The swap market model (SMM) makes it possible to derive Black's formula for swaptions. Moreover, it is possible to apply the LMM to obtain an analytic approximation (known as Rebonato's formula) for the volatility in Black's swaption formula. This facilitates efficient calibration of the LMM.

5.1 LIBOR market model

Consider a set of dates $0 \leq T_0 < T_1 < \cdots < T_n$ with accrual periods $\tau_i = T_i - T_{i-1}$ for $i = 1, \ldots, n$. The forward LIBOR rate $F(t; T_{i-1}, T_i)$ associated with each accrual period τ_i is a simply compounded rate parameterised by three time indices, the present time t, the start of a spot LIBOR rate T_{i-1} and the maturity T_i, where $t \leq T_{i-1} < T_i$. In Section 1.2 we saw that the forward rate can be expressed in terms of zero-coupon bonds as

$$F(t; T_{i-1}, T_i) = \frac{1}{\tau_i} \left(\frac{B(t, T_{i-1})}{B(t, T_i)} - 1 \right).$$

For notational convenience we put

$$F_i(t) = F(t; T_{i-1}, T_i)$$

for $i = 1, \ldots, n$. In this notation $F_i(T_{i-1}) = L(T_{i-1}, T_i)$ is the spot LIBOR rate starting at time T_{i-1} and maturing at T_i (see Figure 5.1). It is common practice to refer to T_{i-1} as the reset date or expiry of the forward rate.

We fix any $j = 1, \ldots, n$ and take $Z_1^j(t), \ldots, Z_n^j(t)$ to be correlated Brownian motions under the forward measure P_{T_j} such that

$$dZ_i^j(t) dZ_k^j(t) = \rho_{i,k} dt \tag{5.1}$$

for each $i, k = 1, \ldots, n$, where $\rho = (\rho_{i,k})_{i,k=1}^n$ is a positive definite symmetric matrix of correlations.

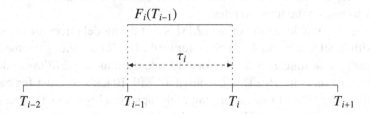

Figure 5.1 Schematic of $F_i(T_{i-1}) = L(T_{i-1}, T_i)$, the spot LIBOR rate between times T_{i-1} and T_i.

In the **LIBOR market model** (LMM) the forward rates $F_i(t)$ are assumed to satisfy an SDE of the form

$$dF_i(t) = \mu_i^j(t)F_i(t)dt + \sigma_i(t)F_i(t)dZ_i^j(t), \tag{5.2}$$

where $\sigma_i(t)$ is a bounded deterministic function for each $i = 1, \ldots, n$. The $\sigma_i(t)$ are called the **instantaneous volatilities** of the forward rates $F_i(t)$, and the $\rho_{i,k}$ the **instantaneous correlations** between $F_i(t)$ and $F_k(t)$.

In Section 5.3 we are going to establish a formula determining the drifts $\mu_i^j(t)$. For the time being, we just consider the particularly simple case when $i = j$. From Section 2.4 we know that $F_i(t)$ is a martingale under the forward measure P_{T_i}. Because $Z_i^i(t)$ is a Brownian motion under P_{T_i}, this means that $\mu_i^i(t) = 0$ and

$$dF_i(t) = \sigma_i(t)F_i(t)dZ_i^i(t). \tag{5.3}$$

Orthogonal Brownian motions

In Section 5.3 we are going to apply the Girsanov theorem to derive a formula for the drifts $\mu_i^j(t)$. One slight difficulty will be that the standard version of the Girsanov theorem (see [BSM]) allows for orthogonal (independent) Brownian motions only, whereas $Z_1^j(t), \ldots, Z_n^j(t)$ are correlated Brownian motions under the forward measure P_{T_j}. To deal with this difficulty we can take $W^j(t) = (W_1^j(t), \ldots, W_n^j(t))$ to be an n-dimensional Brownian motion under P_{T_j} (hence $W_1^j(t), \ldots, W_n^j(t)$ are independent) and put

$$Z_i^j(t) = \sum_{l=1}^{n} \eta_{i,l} W_l^j(t) \quad \text{for each } i = 1, \ldots, n, \tag{5.4}$$

where η is a square root of the correlation matrix ρ, that is, a symmetric matrix η such that

$$\sum_{l=1}^{n} \eta_{i,l}\eta_{k,l} = \rho_{i,k} \quad \text{for each } i,k = 1,\ldots,n. \tag{5.5}$$

It follows that $Z_1^j(t),\ldots,Z_n^j(t)$ are Brownian motions under the forward measure P_{T_j} correlated as in (5.1).

Exercise 5.1 Show that $Z_1^j(t),\ldots,Z_n^j(t)$ given by (5.4) are indeed Brownian motions under the forward measure P_{T_j} such that (5.1) holds.

5.2 Black's caplet formula

The fact that each forward rate $F_i(t)$ can be modelled as a driftless log-normal process under the forward measure P_{T_i} allows us to derive Black's pricing formula for caplets stated in Section 2.9. The ability of the LMM framework to reproduce in a natural way one of the most important market formulae is one of its key features.

Assuming a notional amount $N = 1$, at each T_i for $i = 1,\ldots,n$ the holder of an interest rate cap receives the payoff

$$\tau_i(L(T_{i-1},T_i) - K)^+ = \tau_i(F_i(T_{i-1}) - K)^+,$$

where K is the strike. Hence the price of the ith caplet at time t is

$$\mathbf{Cpl}_i(t) = \tau_i B(t,T_i)\mathbb{E}_{P_{T_i}}\left((F_i(T_{i-1}) - K)^+ \big| \mathcal{F}_t\right),$$

$$= \tau_i B(t,T_i)\left(\mathbb{E}_{P_{T_i}}\left(F_i(T_{i-1})\mathbf{1}_{\{F_i(T_{i-1})\geq K\}}\big| \mathcal{F}_t\right) - K\mathbb{E}_{P_{T_i}}\left(\mathbf{1}_{\{F_i(T_{i-1})\geq K\}}\big| \mathcal{F}_t\right)\right).$$

The forward rate $F_i(t)$ satisfies the SDE (5.3). This can be solved to give

$$F_i(T_{i-1}) = F_i(t)\exp\left(\int_t^{T_{i-1}} \sigma_i(s)dZ_i^i(s) - \frac{1}{2}\int_t^{T_{i-1}} \sigma_i(s)^2 ds\right).$$

Since $\sigma_i(t)$ is a bounded deterministic function and $Z_i^i(t)$ is a Brownian motion under P_{T_i}, the stochastic integral $\int_t^{T_{i-1}} \sigma_i(s)dZ_i^i(s)$ is independent of $\mathcal{F}_t$ and normally distributed with mean 0 and variance $\int_t^{T_{i-1}} \sigma_i(s)^2 ds$. It follows that

$$\mathbb{E}_{P_{T_i}}\left(F_i(T_{i-1})\mathbf{1}_{\{F_i(T_{i-1})\geq K\}}\big| \mathcal{F}_t\right) = F_i(t)N(d_+) \tag{5.6}$$

and

$$\mathbb{E}_{P_{T_i}}\left(\mathbf{1}_{\{F_i(T_{i-1})\geq K\}}\Big|\mathcal{F}_t\right) = N(d_-),\tag{5.7}$$

where

$$d_\pm = \frac{\ln\frac{F_i(t)}{K} \pm \frac{1}{2}\int_t^{T_{i-1}}\sigma_i(s)^2 ds}{\sqrt{\int_t^{T_{i-1}}\sigma_i(s)^2 ds}}$$

and

$$N(x) = \int_{-\infty}^x \frac{1}{\sqrt{2\pi}}e^{-\frac{y^2}{2}}dy,$$

is the standard normal distribution function.

Exercise 5.2   Verify formulae (5.6) and (5.7).

It follows that the price at time t of the ith caplet is

$$\mathbf{Cpl}_i(t) = \tau_i B(t, T_i)(F(t; T_{i-1}, T_i)N(d_+) - KN(d_-)).\tag{5.8}$$

Setting

$$v_i = \sqrt{\frac{1}{T_{i-1}-t}\int_t^{T_{i-1}}\sigma_i(s)^2 ds},\tag{5.9}$$

we recover Black's formula (2.24) for caplets with v_i substituted for the volatility σ, that is, we have

$$\mathbf{Cpl}_i(t) = \mathbf{Cpl}_i^{\mathrm{Black}}(t; v_i).$$

We can think of v_i as the model implied caplet volatility. The caplet price in the LMM will be consistent with the market price when $v_i = \hat{\sigma}_i^{\mathrm{caplet}}$; see Section 2.9.

5.3   Drifts and change of numeraire

In this section we establish formulae for the drifts $\mu_i^j(t)$ in the SDE (5.2) for the forward rate $F_i(t)$. We have already seen in (5.3) that $\mu_i^i(t) = 0$. Hence, using the change of numeraire technique, we can compute $\mu_i^j(t)$ when $i \neq j$. To calculate the drift there are a number of related approaches we can take. Here we apply the Girsanov theorem.

Let $Z_1^j(t), \dots, Z_n^j(t)$ be correlated Brownian motions under the forward measure P_{T_j} such that (5.1) holds. Suppose that $i \le j$. We then have $T_i \le T_j$. By Exercise 2.2, the Radon–Nikodym derivative of P_{T_i} with respect to P_{T_j} is

$$\frac{dP_{T_i}}{dP_{T_j}} = \frac{B(0, T_j)}{B(0, T_i)} \frac{1}{B(T_i, T_j)}.$$

This is related to the change of numeraire from $B(t, T_j)$ to $B(t, T_i)$. The corresponding Radon–Nikodym density process is

$$\xi_j^i(t) = \mathbb{E}_{P_{T_j}}\left(\frac{dP_{T_i}}{dP_{T_j}} \bigg| \mathcal{F}_t \right)$$

$$= \mathbb{E}_{P_{T_j}}\left(\frac{B(0, T_j)}{B(0, T_i)} \frac{B(T_i, T_i)}{B(T_i, T_j)} \bigg| \mathcal{F}_t \right) = \frac{B(0, T_j)}{B(0, T_i)} \frac{B(t, T_i)}{B(t, T_j)}$$

for any $t \in [0, T_i]$. It can be written as

$$\xi_j^i(t) = \frac{B(0, T_j)}{B(0, T_i)} \prod_{k=i+1}^{j} \frac{B(t, T_{k-1})}{B(t, T_k)} = \frac{B(0, T_j)}{B(0, T_i)} \prod_{k=i+1}^{j} (1 + \tau_k F_k(t)).$$

Applying the Itô formula, we get

$$d\xi_j^i(t) = \xi_j^i(t) \sum_{k=i+1}^{j} \frac{\tau_k dF_k(t)}{1 + \tau_k F_k(t)} + (\cdots) dt.$$

The explicit expressions for the terms with dt will not be needed. We substitute

$$dF_k(t) = \mu_k^j(t) F_k(t) dt + \sigma_k(t) F_k(t) dZ_k^j(t)$$

using the SDE (5.2) and collect the terms with $dZ_k^j(t)$ and dt separately. Because $\xi_j^i(t)$ is a martingale under P_{T_j}, the terms with dt cancel out, leaving only those with $dZ_k^j(t)$, so

$$d\xi_j^i(t) = \xi_j^i(t) \sum_{k=i+1}^{j} \frac{\tau_k \sigma_k(t) F_k(t)}{1 + \tau_k F_k(t)} dZ_k^j(t). \tag{5.10}$$

Next, substituting for $Z_k^j(t)$ from (5.4), we get

$$d\xi_j^i(t) = \xi_j^i(t) \sum_{k=i+1}^{j} \sum_{l=1}^{n} \frac{\tau_k \sigma_k(t) F_k(t)}{1 + \tau_k F_k(t)} \eta_{k,l} dW_l^j(t),$$

and solve this SDE to obtain

$$\xi_j^i(t) = \exp\left(\int_0^t \sum_{k=i+1}^{j} \sum_{l=1}^{n} \frac{\tau_k \sigma_k(s) F_k(s)}{1 + \tau_k F_k(s)} \eta_{k,l} dW_l^j(s)\right.$$
$$\left. - \frac{1}{2} \int_0^t \sum_{k=i+1}^{j} \sum_{l=i+1}^{j} \frac{\tau_k \sigma_k(s) F_k(s)}{1 + \tau_k F_k(s)} \frac{\tau_l \sigma_l(s) F_l(s)}{1 + \tau_l F_l(s)} \rho_{k,l} ds\right).$$

Given that $W_l^j(t)$ for $l = 1, \ldots, n$ are the components of an n-dimensional Brownian motion under the forward measure P_{T_j}, we can apply the Girsanov theorem (see [BSM]) to conclude that

$$W_l^i(t) = W_l^j(t) - \int_0^t \sum_{k=i+1}^{j} \frac{\tau_k \sigma_k(s) F_k(s)}{1 + \tau_k F_k(s)} \eta_{k,l} ds$$

for $l = 1, \ldots, n$ are the components of an n-dimensional Brownian motion under P_{T_i}. Now we apply (5.4) once again together with (5.5) to finally find using Exercise 5.1 that

$$Z_l^i(t) = \sum_{m=1}^{n} \eta_{l,m} W_m^i(t) = \sum_{m=1}^{n} \eta_{l,m} \left(W_m^j(t) - \int_0^t \sum_{k=i+1}^{j} \frac{\tau_k \sigma_k(s) F_k(s)}{1 + \tau_k F_k(s)} \eta_{k,m} ds\right)$$
$$= Z_l^j(t) - \int_0^t \sum_{k=i+1}^{j} \frac{\tau_k \sigma_k(s) F_k(s)}{1 + \tau_k F_k(s)} \rho_{k,l} ds$$

for $l = 1, \ldots, n$ are Brownian motions under P_{T_i} correlated so that

$$dZ_k^i(t) dZ_l^i(t) = \rho_{k,l} dt. \qquad (5.11)$$

We have proved the following proposition.

Proposition 5.1
Let $Z_1^j(t), \ldots, Z_n^j(t)$ be correlated Brownian motions under P_{T_j} satisfying (5.1). Then for any $i \leq j$

$$Z_l^i(t) = Z_l^j(t) - \int_0^t \sum_{k=i+1}^{j} \frac{\tau_k \sigma_k(s) F_k(s)}{1 + \tau_k F_k(s)} \rho_{k,l} ds,$$

where $l = 1, \ldots, n$, are correlated Brownian motions under P_{T_i} such that (5.11) holds.

As a consequence of Proposition 5.1, we obtain the important result that the drifts $\mu_i^j(t)$ of the forward rates $F_i(t)$ are uniquely determined by the following formulae.

Theorem 5.2

The drifts $\mu_i^j(t)$ of the forward rates $F_i(t)$ in (5.2) are given by

$$
\mu_i^j(t) = \begin{cases}
-\displaystyle\sum_{k=i+1}^{j} \frac{\tau_k \rho_{k,i} \sigma_i(t) \sigma_k(t) F_k(t)}{1 + \tau_k F_k(t)} & \text{when } i < j, \\[4mm]
0 & \text{when } i = j, \\[4mm]
\displaystyle\sum_{k=j+1}^{i} \frac{\tau_k \rho_{k,i} \sigma_i(t) \sigma_k(t) F_k(t)}{1 + \tau_k F_k(t)} & \text{when } i > j.
\end{cases}
$$

Proof The case when $i = j$ was covered in (5.3). If $i < j$, we can apply Proposition 5.1 with $l = i$ to get

$$
Z_i^i(t) = Z_i^j(t) - \int_0^t \sum_{k=i+1}^{j} \frac{\tau_k \sigma_k(s) F_k(s)}{1 + \tau_k F_k(s)} \rho_{k,i} ds.
$$

We substitute this into (5.3) and obtain

$$
dF_i(t) = \sigma_i(t) F_i(t) dZ_i^i(t)
$$

$$
= \sigma_i(t) F_i(t) dZ_i^j(t) - \sigma_i(t) F_i(t) \sum_{k=i+1}^{j} \frac{\tau_k \sigma_k(t) F_k(t)}{1 + \tau_k F_k(t)} \rho_{k,i} dt.
$$

Comparing this with (5.2), we arrive at the formula for $\mu_i^j(t)$. The case when $i > j$ is left as an exercise. $\qquad\square$

Exercise 5.3 Let $Z_1^j(t), \ldots, Z_n^j(t)$ be correlated Brownian motions under P_{T_j} satisfying (5.1). Show that for any $i \geq j$

$$
Z_i^i(t) = Z_i^j(t) + \int_0^t \sum_{k=j+1}^{i} \frac{\tau_k \sigma_k(s) F_k(s)}{1 + \tau_k F_k(s)} \rho_{k,l} ds,
$$

where $l = 1, \ldots, n$, are correlated Brownian motions under P_{T_i} such that (5.11) holds.

Exercise 5.4 Verify the formula for $\mu_i^j(t)$ in Theorem 5.2 when $i > j$.

5.4 Terminal measure

A popular choice of numeraire is the zero-coupon bond $B(t, T_n)$ maturing at time T_n. The associated measure P_{T_n} is known as the **terminal measure**. It follows from Theorem 5.2 that

$$dF_i(t) = \mu_i^n(t)F_i(t)dt + \sigma_i(t)F_i(t)dZ_i^n(t) \qquad (5.12)$$

with

$$\mu_i^n(t) = -\sum_{k=i+1}^{n} \frac{\tau_k \rho_{k,i}\sigma_i(t)\sigma_k(t)F_k(t)}{1 + \tau_k F_k(t)} \qquad (5.13)$$

for $i = 1, \ldots, n$, where $Z_1^n(t), \ldots, Z_n^n(t)$ are correlated Brownian motions under the terminal measure P_{T_n} such that for all $i, j = 1, \ldots, n$

$$dZ_i^n(t)dZ_j^n(t) = \rho_{i,j}dt. \qquad (5.14)$$

5.5 Spot LIBOR measure

We are going to construct a discrete analogue of the money market account. At time 0 we begin by investing one dollar to buy an amount $B(0, T_0)^{-1}$ of T_0-bonds. At time T_0 the bonds will be worth $B(0, T_0)^{-1}$, which we reinvest to buy an amount $B(0, T_0)^{-1}B(T_0, T_1)^{-1}$ of T_1-bonds. We continue in this way, reinvesting the proceeds at each date T_{i-1} into zero-coupon bonds maturing at the next date T_i for $i = 1, \ldots, n$. For any $t \in [0, T_n]$, let $\alpha(t)$ denote the index of the next reset date at time t, that is,

$$\alpha(t) = \min\{j : t \le T_j, \ j = 0, \ldots, n\}. \qquad (5.15)$$

The value of our bond portfolio at time t will be

$$L(t) = B(t, T_{\alpha(t)})\prod_{k=0}^{\alpha(t)} \frac{1}{B(T_{k-1}, T_k)},$$

where we put $T_{-1} = 0$ for notational simplicity. We call $L(t)$ the **discrete money market account**.

Exercise 5.5 Show that $L(t)$ discounted by $B(t, T_n)$ is a martingale under the terminal measure P_{T_n}, and $L(t)$ discounted by $B(t)$ is a martingale under the risk-neutral measure Q.

The measure corresponding to the choice of $L(t)$ as numeraire is called the **spot LIBOR measure** and will be denoted by P_L. The Radon–Nikodym derivative of P_L with respect to the terminal measure P_{T_n} is (see Section 2.1)

$$\frac{dP_L}{dP_{T_n}} = \frac{B(0, T_n)}{L(0)} \frac{L(T_n)}{B(T_n, T_n)} = B(0, T_n)L(T_n).$$

Observe that $B(0, T_n)L(T_n)$ is an $\mathcal{F}_{T_{n-1}}$-measurable random variable, hence P_L is defined on the σ-field $\mathcal{F}_{T_{n-1}}$.

We are going to show that the forward rates satisfy an SDE of the form

$$dF_i(t) = \mu_i^L(t)F_i(t)dt + \sigma_i(t)F_i(t)dZ_i^L(t), \tag{5.16}$$

where $Z_1^L(t), \ldots, Z_n^L(t)$ are correlated Brownian motions under P_L such that for each $i, j = 1, \ldots, n$

$$dZ_i^L(t)dZ_j^L(t) = \rho_{i,j}dt,$$

and we shall derive a formula for the drift $\mu_i^L(t)$.

We proceed in a similar fashion as in Section 5.3. Take $Z_1^n(t), \ldots, Z_n^n(t)$ to be correlated Brownian motions under the terminal measure P_{T_n} that satisfy (5.14) and consider the Radon–Nikodym density process

$$\xi_n^L(t) = \mathbb{E}_{P_{T_n}}\left(\frac{dP_L}{dP_{T_n}}\bigg| \mathcal{F}_t\right) = \mathbb{E}_{P_{T_n}}(B(0, T_n)L(T_n)| \mathcal{F}_t)$$

$$= B(0, T_n)\mathbb{E}_{P_{T_n}}\left(\frac{L(T_n)}{B(T_n, T_n)}\bigg| \mathcal{F}_t\right) = B(0, T_n)\frac{L(t)}{B(t, T_n)}.$$

The last equality holds since $L(t)$ discounted by $B(t, T_n)$ is a martingale under P_{T_n} according to Exercise 5.5. Observe that for each $t \in [0, T_{n-1}]$

$$L(t) = B(t, T_{\alpha(t)})L(T_{\alpha(t)}),$$

and so

$$\xi_n^L(t) = B(0, T_n)L(T_{\alpha(t)})\frac{B(t, T_{\alpha(t)})}{B(t, T_n)} = B(0, T_n)L(T_{\alpha(t)}) \prod_{k=\alpha(t)+1}^{n} \frac{B(t, T_{k-1})}{B(t, T_k)}$$

$$= B(0, T_n)L(T_{\alpha(t)}) \prod_{k=\alpha(t)+1}^{n} (1 + \tau_k F_k(t)).$$

Just like in Section 5.3, it follows that

$$d\xi_n^L(t) = \xi_n^L(t) \sum_{k=\alpha(t)+1}^{n} \frac{\tau_k dF_k(t)}{1 + \tau_k F_k(t)} + (\cdots)dt.$$

Expressing $dF_k(t)$ by means of (5.12) and using the fact that $\xi_i^L(t)$ is a martingale under P_L, we find that all terms in dt will cancel. This gives

$$d\xi_n^L(t) = \xi_n^L(t) \sum_{k=\alpha(t)+1}^{n} \frac{\tau_k \sigma_k(t) F_k(t)}{1 + \tau_k F_k(t)} dZ_k^n(t).$$

The same argument as in Section 5.3, involving orthogonal Brownian motions and the Girsanov theorem, then shows that

$$Z_i^L(t) = Z_i^n(t) - \int_0^t \sum_{k=\alpha(t)+1}^{n} \frac{\tau_k \sigma_k(s) F_k(s)}{1 + \tau_k F_k(s)} \rho_{k,i} ds \qquad (5.17)$$

for $i = 1,\ldots,n$ are correlated Brownian motions under the spot LIBOR measure P_L such that

$$dZ_i^L(t)dZ_j^L(t) = \rho_{i,j}dt.$$

Hence we arrive at the following result.

Proposition 5.3
The forward rates $F_i(t)$ satisfy the SDE (5.16) with drift

$$\mu_i^L(t) = \sum_{k=\alpha(t)+1}^{i} \frac{\tau_k \rho_{k,i} \sigma_i(t) \sigma_k(t) F_k(t)}{1 + \tau_k F_k(t)}$$

for any $i = 1,\ldots,n$ and $t \in [0, T_{i-1}]$, where $\alpha(t)$ denotes the index of the next reset date at time t given by (5.15).

Proof Using (5.17) to replace $Z_i^n(t)$ in (5.12) by $Z_i^L(t)$, we get

$$dF_i(t) = -\sum_{k=i+1}^{n} \frac{\tau_k \rho_{k,i} \sigma_i(t) \sigma_k(t) F_i(t) F_k(t)}{1 + \tau_k F_k(t)} dt + \sigma_i(t) F_i(t) dZ_i^n(t)$$

$$= -\sum_{k=i+1}^{n} \frac{\tau_k \rho_{k,i} \sigma_i(t) \sigma_k(t) F_i(t) F_k(t)}{1 + \tau_k F_k(t)} dt$$

$$+ \sigma_i(t) F_i(t) \left(\sum_{k=\alpha(t)+1}^{n} \frac{\tau_k \sigma_k(t) F_k(t)}{1 + \tau_k F_k(t)} \rho_{k,i} dt + dZ_i^L(t) \right)$$

$$= \sum_{k=\alpha(t)+1}^{i} \frac{\tau_k \rho_{k,i} \sigma_i(t) \sigma_k(t) F_i(t) F_k(t)}{1 + \tau_k F_k(t)} dt + \sigma_i(t) F_i(t) dZ_i^L(t).$$

This shows that $F_i(t)$ satisfies (5.16) with drift $\mu_i^L(t)$ as stated in the proposition. $\qquad\square$

Remark 5.4

In the LMM we need to discretise the continuous-time dynamics if we wish to model a given derivative. This will introduce a bias in the forward rates, which depends on the number of terms in the drift summation. From (5.12) we can see that, under the terminal measure P_{T_n}, the drift of a given forward rate $F_i(t)$ contains $n - i$ terms in the summation. However, under the spot LIBOR measure P_L, the number of terms in the summation is time dependent. In fact for $T_{i-2} \le t < T_{i-1}$ there is just one term. Therefore, under the spot LIBOR measure the bias is more evenly spread between the different rates.

5.6 Brace–Gątarek–Musiela approach

The approach due to Brace, Gątarek and Musiela is to write the SDE for the forward rates $F_i(t)$ in terms of Brownian motions under the risk-neutral measure Q and to derive a formula for the drifts by working within the HJM framework.

To this end it is convenient to write the SDE (5.2) for the forward rates $F_i(t)$ in terms of orthogonal rather than correlated Brownian motions. Substituting (5.4) into (5.2), we get

$$dF_i(t) = \mu_i^j(t)F_i(t)dt + F_i(t) \sum_{k=1}^{n} \lambda_{i,k}(t)dW_k^j(t), \qquad (5.18)$$

where

$$\lambda_{i,k}(t) = \sigma_i(t)\eta_{i,k}$$

for $i, k = 1, \ldots, n$, and where $(W_1^j(t), \ldots, W_n^j(t))$ is an n-dimensional Brownian motion under the forward measure P_{T_j}.

In Section 2.6, formula (2.14), we related a one-dimensional Brownian motion under the risk-neutral measure Q to a one-dimensional Brownian motion under the forward measure P_S by means of the Girsanov theorem. This argument can be extended to multi-dimensional Brownian motions.

Exercise 5.6 Let $(W_1(t), \ldots, W_n(t))$ be an n-dimensional Brownian motion under the risk-neutral measure Q. Show that

$(W_1^S(t), \ldots, W_n^S(t))$, where

$$W_k^S(t) = W_k(t) - \int_0^t \Sigma_k(u, S)\,du \quad \text{for } k = 1, \ldots, n \text{ and } t \in [0, S],$$

is an n-dimensional Brownian motion under the forward measure P_S.

It follows from this exercise that $(W_1^j(t), \ldots, W_n^j(t))$, where

$$W_k^j(t) = W_k(t) - \int_0^t \Sigma_k(u, T_j)\,du \quad \text{for } k = 1, \ldots, n \text{ and } t \in [0, T_j],$$

in an n-dimensional Brownian motion under P_{T_j}. Substituting this into (5.18) where we set $j = i$ and use the fact that $\mu_i^i(t) = 0$, we find that

$$dF_i(t) = \mu_i(t)F_i(t)dt + F_i(t) \sum_{k=1}^n \lambda_{i,k}(t)dW_k(t), \qquad (5.19)$$

where

$$\mu_i(t) = -\sum_{k=1}^n \lambda_{i,k}(t)\Sigma_k(t, T_i),$$

and where (by an argument similar to that in Exercise 5.1)

$$Z_i(t) = \sum_{l=1}^n \eta_{i,l} W_l(t)$$

for $i = 1, \ldots, n$ are correlated Brownian motions under the risk-neutral measure Q such that

$$dZ_i(t)dZ_j(t) = \rho_{i,j}dt.$$

Now recall that the zero-coupon bond price process in a multi-factor HJM model evolves according to

$$dB(t, T) = r(t)B(t, T)dt + \sum_{k=1}^n \Sigma_k(t, T)B(t, T)dW_k(t),$$

where $(W_1(t), \ldots, W_n(t))$ is an n-dimensional Brownian motion under the risk-neutral measure Q and

$$\Sigma_k(t, T) = -\int_t^T \sigma_k(t, u)\,du,$$

with $\sigma_k(t, T)$ for $k = 1, \ldots, n$ being the volatilities of the instantaneous forward rate $f(t, T)$; see Theorem 4.6.

Applying the Itô formula to

$$F_i(t) = \frac{1}{\tau_i}\left(\frac{B(t,T_{i-1})}{B(t,T_i)} - 1\right),$$

we can find that

$$dF_i(t) = \frac{1}{\tau_i}\frac{dB(t,T_{i-1})}{B(t,T_i)} + \frac{1}{\tau_i}B(t,T_{i-1})d\left(\frac{1}{B(t,T_i)}\right) + \frac{1}{\tau_i}dB(t,T_{i-1})d\left(\frac{1}{B(t,T_i)}\right)$$

$$= \frac{1+\tau_i F_i(t)}{\tau_i}\sum_{k=1}^{n}\Sigma_k(t,T_i)\left(\Sigma_k(t,T_i) - \Sigma_k(t,T_{i-1})\right)dt$$

$$+ \frac{1+\tau_i F_i(t)}{\tau_i}\sum_{k=1}^{n}\left(\Sigma_k(t,T_{i-1}) - \Sigma_k(t,T_i)\right)dW_k(t).$$

By comparing the coefficients in front of $dW_k(t)$ in the above expressions for $dF_i(t)$, we conclude that

$$\Sigma_k(t,T_i) = \Sigma_k(t,T_{i-1}) - \frac{\tau_i F_i(t)}{1+\tau_i F_i(t)}\lambda_{i,k}(t)$$

for each i such that $t \le T_{i-1}$. The last relationship can be iterated until we reach the smallest index j such that $t \le T_j$, which as before will be denoted by $\alpha(t)$; see (5.15). Namely,

$$\Sigma_k(t,T_i) = \Sigma_k(t,T_{i-1}) - \frac{\tau_i F_i(t)}{1+\tau_i F_i(t)}\lambda_{i,k}(t)$$

$$= \Sigma_k(t,T_{i-2}) - \frac{\tau_i F_i(t)}{1+\tau_i F_i(t)}\lambda_{i,k}(t) - \frac{\tau_{i-1}F_{i-1}(t)}{1+\tau_{i-1}F_{i-1}(t)}\lambda_{i-1,k}(t)$$

$$\vdots$$

$$= \Sigma_k(t,T_{\alpha(t)}) - \sum_{l=\alpha(t)+1}^{i}\frac{\tau_l F_l(t)}{1+\tau_l F_l(t)}\lambda_{l,k}(t). \qquad (5.20)$$

Substituting this into the formula for $\mu_i(t)$, we get

$$\mu_i(t) = -\sum_{k=1}^{n}\lambda_{i,k}(t)\Sigma_k(t,T_i)$$

$$= -\sum_{k=1}^{n}\lambda_{i,k}(t)\Sigma_k(t,T_{\alpha(t)}) + \sum_{l=\alpha(t)+1}^{i}\frac{\tau_l F_l(t)}{1+\tau_l F_l(t)}\sum_{k=1}^{n}\lambda_{i,k}(t)\lambda_{l,k}(t)$$

$$= \sum_{k=1}^{n}\lambda_{i,k}(t)\int_{t}^{T_{\alpha(t)}}\sigma_k(t,u)du + \sum_{l=\alpha(t)+1}^{i}\frac{\tau_l\rho_{i,l}\sigma_i(t)\sigma_l(t)F_l(t)}{1+\tau_l F_l(t)}. \qquad (5.21)$$

We have proved the following result.

Proposition 5.5
The forward rates $F_i(t)$ satisfy the SDE

$$dF_i(t) = \mu_i(t)F_i(t)dt + \sigma_i(t)F_i(t)dZ_i(t),$$

where $Z_1(t), \ldots, Z_n(t)$ are correlated Brownian motions under the risk-neutral measure Q such that

$$dZ_i(t)dZ_j(t) = \rho_{i,j}dt,$$

and where the drifts $\mu_i(t)$ are given by (5.21).

Remark 5.6
Note that the first term in (5.21) contains the instantaneous forward-rate volatilities $\sigma_k(t, u)$. The need to model these volatilities complicates the formula for the drift. Brace, Gątarek and Musiela make the simplifying assumption that $\Sigma_k(t, T_{\alpha(t)}) = 0$. Under this assumption the SDE for the forward rate under the risk-neutral measure Q can be written as

$$dF_i(t) = \sum_{l=\alpha(t)+1}^{i} \frac{\tau_l \rho_{i,l}\sigma_i(t)\sigma_l(t)F_l(t)}{1 + \tau_l F_l(t)} F_i(t)dt + \sigma_i(t)F_i(t)dZ_i(t).$$

The following exercises show that the same formula for the drift applies without the need for the above simplifying assumption when working under the spot LIBOR measure P_L instead of the risk-neutral measure Q.

Exercise 5.7 Show that for all $k = 1, \ldots, n$ and $t \in [0, T_i]$

$$W_k^i(t) = W_k^L(t) - \int_0^t \left(\Sigma_k(s, T_i) - \Sigma_k(s, T_{\alpha(t)}) \right) ds, \qquad (5.22)$$

where $(W_1^L(t), \ldots, W_n^L(t))$ and $(W_1^i(t), \ldots, W_n^i(t))$ are n-dimensional Brownian motions under the spot LIBOR measure P_L and under the forward measure P_{T_i}, respectively.

Exercise 5.8 Using (5.22), show that the correlated Brownian motions

$$Z_j^i(t) = \sum_{k=1}^{n} \eta_{j,k} W_k^i(t), \quad Z_j^L(t) = \sum_{k=1}^{n} \eta_{j,k} W_k^L(t)$$

under the spot LIBOR measure P_L and under the forward measure P_{T_i}, respectively, are related by

$$Z_j^i(t) = Z_j^L(t) + \int_0^t \sum_{k=\alpha(t)+1}^i \frac{\tau_k \rho_{j,k} \sigma_k(s) F_k(s)}{1 + \tau_k F_k(s)} ds \qquad (5.23)$$

for all $j = 1, \ldots, n$ and $t \in [0, T_i]$.

Exercise 5.9 Using (5.23), show that the forward rates satisfy the SDE

$$dF_i(t) = \sum_{k=\alpha(t)+1}^i \frac{\tau_k \rho_{i,k} \sigma_i(t) \sigma_k(t) F_k(t)}{1 + \tau_k F_k(t)} F_i(t) dt + \sigma_i(t) F_i(t) dZ_i^L(t),$$

which is consistent with Proposition 5.3.

5.7 Instantaneous volatility

Much like the HJM model, the LMM is really a modelling framework rather than a fully formed model. To specify a concrete model we need to choose the form of both the instantaneous volatility and a correlation structure between the different forward rates. Then we need to calibrate the model to market data. In Section 5.2 we saw a direct link between the implied volatility in Black's formula for a caplet and the instantaneous volatility of the LMM formulation.

Piecewise constant form

For simplicity, we can assume that the instantaneous volatility $\sigma_i(t)$ of the forward rate $F_i(t)$ is constant over each accrual period and depends exclusively on the number of reset dates in the time interval $[t, T_{i-1}]$. This gives

$$\sigma_i(t) = \sigma_{i-\alpha(t)}, \qquad (5.24)$$

where $\alpha(t)$ denotes the index of the next reset date defined by (5.15).

In Table 5.1 we can see that the volatility structure of the forward rates $F_1(t), \ldots, F_n(t)$ is described by n constant parameters $\sigma_1, \ldots, \sigma_n$. Note that the forward LIBOR rate $F_i(t)$ will have already expired for $t > T_{i-1}$.

Table 5.1 *Instantaneous volatilities for the time-homogeneous piecewise constant formulation* (5.24).

	$(0, T_0]$	$(T_0, T_1]$	$(T_1, T_2]$	$\cdots$	$(T_{n-2}, T_{n-1}]$
$F_1(t)$	σ_1	expired		$\cdots$	
$F_2(t)$	σ_2	σ_1	expired	$\cdots$	
$\cdots$	$\cdots$	$\cdots$	$\cdots$	$\cdots$	
$F_n(t)$	σ_n	σ_{n-1}	σ_{n-2}	$\cdots$	σ_1

Because the instantaneous volatility depends on time t only via the remaining number of reset dates, the choice (5.24) is referred to as a time-homogeneous form for the volatility. There is a sound reason why we would wish to avoid having an explicit dependence on t. A financially plausible model should allow for a stationary volatility term structure.

Another feature we need to account for is that in 'normal' market conditions the graph of the volatility term structure is typically hump shaped. The implied volatility is upward sloping for maturities out to two–three years and then falls gradually for caps with a longer time to maturity. However, in general, a time-homogeneous form is too inflexible to allow for an accurate fit to a typical hump-shaped term structure. With this in mind, we modify (5.24) by introducing constant parameters κ_i depending solely on the maturity of the ith forward rate,

$$\sigma_i(t) = \kappa_i \sigma_{i-\alpha(t)}.$$

If the κ_i are chosen so that they are close to one, the above form for the instantaneous volatility is approximately time homogenous.

Parametric form

An alternative to the piecewise constant form is to choose some parametric form for the instantaneous volatility. A popular parametric form that is both time homogenous (in the sense that it depends on t via the time to expiry $T_{i-1} - t$) and allows for a hump-shaped volatility is

$$\sigma_i(t) = (a + b(T_{i-1} - t))e^{-c(T_{i-1}-t)} + d, \qquad (5.25)$$

where a, b, c and d are constants and $c > 0$.

An appropriate choice of parameters leads to a curve with low volatility

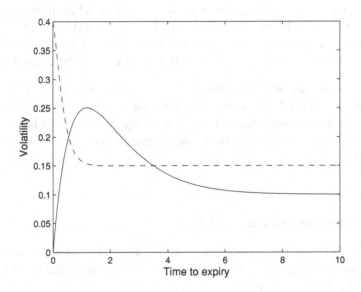

Figure 5.2 The hump-shaped curve (solid line) is given by (5.25) with parameters $a = -0.1$, $b = 0.5$, $c = 1$, $d = 0.1$. The dashed line is obtained with $a = 0.25$, $b = 1$, $c = 5$, $d = 0.15$.

for forward rates with a long time to expiry, peaking at around two years to expiry, and then falling again as the rates are about to reset. Examining the behaviour of (5.25) as $T_{i-1} - t$ tends to zero and as $T_{i-1} - t$ tends to infinity, we can see that $a + d$ is the instantaneous volatility of a forward rate for very short expiry times, while d is the volatility for very long expiry times. We must choose parameters such that $a + d > 0$ and $d > 0$. The extremum of (5.25) (when written as a function of time to expiry $T_{i-1} - t$) is given by $\frac{1}{c} - \frac{a}{b}$, and it is a maximum if $b > 0$ (see Exercise 5.10). In 'normal' market conditions the parameters should give rise to a hump-shaped curve as depicted in Figure 5.2, where the maximum occurs between one and two years to expiry.

Exercise 5.10 Show that the extremum of the instantaneous volatility (5.25) is attained when the time to expiry is $T_{i-1} - t = \frac{1}{c} - \frac{a}{b}$, and that it is a maximum if $b > 0$.

Remark 5.7
What constitutes normal market conditions is open to debate, particularly

since the credit crisis, where the implied volatility could be at its highest for short expiries. Fortunately, for a certain range of parameters, (5.25) is monotonically decaying (see the dashed line in Figure 5.2), so is capable of reproducing the volatility term structure observed since the credit crisis.

As was the case with the time-homogeneous piecewise constant function (5.24), we need to modify (5.25) if we are to provide an accurate fit to market data. Issues relating to calibration are discussed in Chapter 6, where we focus our attention on the parametric form of the instantaneous volatility.

5.8 Instantaneous correlation

In the LMM (5.2), the instantaneous correlation between the forward rates $F_i(t)$ and $F_j(t)$ is denoted by $\rho_{i,j}$. The correlation matrix for the set of forward rates $F_1(t), \ldots, F_n(t)$ is $\rho = (\rho_{i,j})_{i,j=1}^n$.

For reasons of tractability it is desirable to describe ρ in terms of some parsimonious parametric form. We then need to fit the model parameters to a sample correlation matrix estimated using historical data. This is significantly different from the approach taken for the instantaneous volatilities, where we calibrate to the prices (or equivalently to the implied volatilities) of actively traded options. In general, it is difficult to extract information about the correlation function from the market prices of European swaptions. Swaptions are far more dependent on the functional form of the instantaneous volatilities than the qualitative shape of the correlation matrix.

We are going to examine the steps involved in estimating the correlation matrix ρ from historical data and then use the results to motivate some simple parametric form for ρ.

Empirical estimation of the correlation matrix

To begin estimating a correlation structure we first need a daily time series of forward LIBOR rates.

Example 5.8
For the US dollar the forward LIBOR rates can be derived by bootstrapping a set of mid-market spot-starting swap rates for maturities

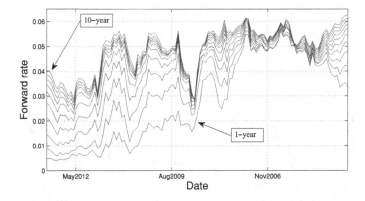

Figure 5.3 USD forward rates between 31 July 2004 and 15 Mar 2013. The time series labelled '1-year' and '10-year' represent the forward rates expiring in one year and 10 years, respectively. The forward rates are derived from mid-market spot-starting swap rates downloaded from the US Federal Reserve website.

$1, 2, 3, 4, 5, 6, 7, 10$ and 30 years. Before we perform the bootstrapping procedure, however, it is necessary to apply cubic spline interpolation between market spot rates to get an estimate of intermediate rates not present in the data.

The next step is to use the time series of LIBOR forward rates to create a sample correlation matrix. The matrix presented in Figure 5.4 is calculated by taking the correlation between log-changes in the forward-rate time series. In the forward-rate time series in Figure 5.3 used to calculate the correlation matrix the time-to-expiry is fixed (constant residual time to expiry) while the expiry date varies. In Figure 5.3 we plot the USD forward rates (with one-year tenor) for expiries of one, two, out to 10 years. For clarity we do not plot the USD rates for expiries of 11 out to 20 years.

Another approach is to use a forward-rate time series where the expiry of each forward rate is fixed and the time-to-expiry decreases while moving through time. In this approach only one year of data is used to construct the correlation matrix since the first forward rate expires in one year.

The sample correlation matrix is difficult to interpret at first glance. Owing to statistical noise the matrix is bound to contain some spurious correlations. Also, the market data we use to derive the forward LIBOR

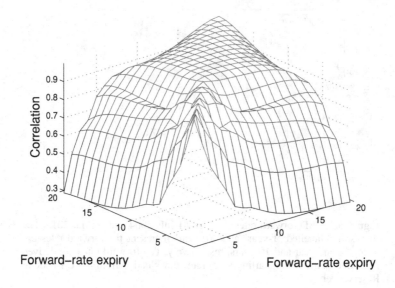

Figure 5.4 Sample correlation matrix for forward rate data in Figure 5.3.

rates should consist only of liquid instruments (those with a tight bid/ask spread). However, the one-year swap rate is not actively traded, and this will affect the correlations between the first forward rate and the later ones.

There are, nonetheless, a number of qualitative features we can observe in Figure 5.4. We would expect all correlations to be positive, and this is confirmed by Figure 5.4. Secondly, it is sensible to assume that the correlation between the first forward rate (expiring in one year) and the forward rates expiring in two, three, ... years should be a monotonically decreasing function. Again, this is broadly supported by the data. Moreover, as we can see in Figure 5.4, this function has a convex shape. We would also expect the correlation between the forward rate expiring in one year and the rate expiring in two years to be less than the correlation between the rate expiring in 19 years and that expiring in 20 years. Returning to Figure 5.4, we can see that for later expiring rates, for example the correlation between the forward rate expiring in 20 years and the rates expiring in $19, 18, \ldots$ years, the correlation is a monotonically decreasing function, but this time with an (approximately) concave shape.

In summary, we conclude that for a fixed i the correlation $\rho_{i,j}$ is a decreasing function of j, where $j > i$. For $i = 1$ this function should have a convex shape, and as i increases the function should become less convex.

Remark 5.9
We should be mindful of the fact that, during a major market event such as the credit crisis, the correlation between the forward rates can change markedly. Unfortunately, estimates based on historical data can be slow to respond to such sudden changes.

Parametric form for the correlation matrix

There are a number of approaches one could take to modelling the above empirical correlation structure in a parsimonious way. A standard approach is to use a decaying exponential to model the correlation matrix with the assumption that the correlation between LIBOR rates $F_i(t)$ and $F_j(t)$ is a function of the time between resets $|T_{i-1} - T_{j-1}|$,

$$\rho_{i,j} = \exp(-\beta|T_{i-1} - T_{j-1}|), \tag{5.26}$$

where $\beta > 0$. In (5.26) the correlation between the first forward rate and the later expiring rates tends to zero asymptotically. Typically, we want to assume some non-zero finite value $\rho_\infty > 0$ for this asymptotic correlation. We can incorporate this assumption by rewriting (5.26) as

$$\rho_{i,j} = \rho_\infty + (1 - \rho_\infty)\exp(-\beta|T_{i-1} - T_{j-1}|).$$

For any positive β the corresponding correlation matrix ρ is symmetric and positive definite. It satisfies the first two empirical observations, namely the correlations are positive, and for a given forward rate $F_i(t)$ with fixed expiry T_{i-1} the correlation decreases as we increase the expiry T_{j-1} of the second rate. However, it does not capture the changes in convexity we observe empirically. In other words, (5.26) does not satisfy the requirement that the correlation between a one-year rate and a two-year rate should be less than that between, say, a 19-year rate and a 20-year rate. For vanilla instruments such as European swaptions (5.26) this is adequate. However, many exotic options are sensitive to the actual shape of the correlation. We need to introduce some dependence on the expiry dates T_{i-1}, T_{j-1} rather than just on $|T_{i-1} - T_{j-1}|$.

With the above issue in mind, practitioners use the following extension to (5.26):

$$\rho_{i,j} = \rho_\infty + (1 - \rho_\infty)\exp(-\beta|(T_{i-1} - t)^\alpha - (T_{j-1} - t)^\alpha|), \tag{5.27}$$

where $t \leq \min(T_{i-1}, T_{j-1})$ and α is a positive constant. However, for a given set of parameters α, β and ρ_∞ this is not guaranteed to lead to a positive definite correlation matrix.

Remark 5.10

Note that $\rho_{i,j}$ given by (5.27) depends on t and as such falls outside the scope of the LMM framework adopted in Section 5.1, where the correlations $\rho_{i,j}$ are assumed to be constant (independent of t). Nonetheless, it is possible to extend the LMM to include time-dependent correlations.

The following procedure for constructing a correlation matrix is consistent with the empirical observations, and the matrix is guaranteed to be positive definite and symmetric. The correlation matrix of the set of forward rates $F_1(t), \ldots, F_n(t)$ is parameterised by $n-1$ constants, denoted by $a_k \in [-1, 1]$ for $k = 1, \ldots, n-1$,

$$\rho = \begin{bmatrix} 1 & a_1 & a_1 a_2 & \cdots & \prod_{k=1}^{n-1} a_k \\ a_1 & 1 & a_2 & \cdots & \prod_{k=2}^{n-1} a_k \\ a_1 a_2 & a_2 & 1 & \cdots & \prod_{k=3}^{n-1} a_k \\ \vdots & \vdots & \vdots & \ddots & \vdots \\ \prod_{k=1}^{n-1} a_k & \prod_{k=2}^{n-1} a_k & \prod_{k=3}^{n-1} a_k & \cdots & 1 \end{bmatrix}. \qquad (5.28)$$

To specify the correlation structure we need to choose some parametric form for a_k. A good choice is a decaying exponential of the form

$$a_k = \exp(-\beta_k(T_k - T_{k-1})), \qquad (5.29)$$

where $\beta_k > 0$ for each k. This choice guarantees that $0 < a_k \leq 1$.

To get the correct empirical behaviour we choose a functional form for β_k that is decreasing in k. We also need to ensure that $\beta_k > 0$ for each k. To give a simple example we can take

$$\beta_k = \frac{\alpha}{k^\gamma}, \qquad (5.30)$$

where α and γ are constants.

Example 5.11

Finally, we calibrate to the sample correlation matrix in Figure 5.4. The resulting matrix is shown in Figure 5.5. We get a smooth correlation surface,

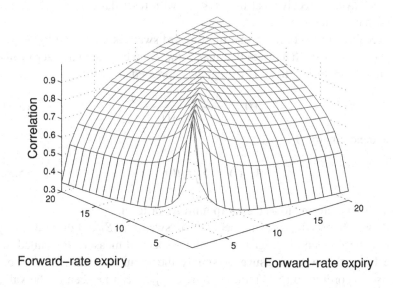

Figure 5.5 Correlation matrix (5.28) with a_k, β_k given by (5.29), (5.30), calibrated to the sample correlation matrix in Figure 5.4. The parameters are $\alpha = 0.441$ and $\gamma = 1.383$.

which retains the key empirical features. Note that the sample correlation matrix in Figure 5.4 may not necessarily be positive definite, but the one constructed in Figure 5.5 is guaranteed to be.

In Chapter 6 we will see that for reasons of numerical efficiency we would typically not use the LMM formulation (5.2) whose correlation structure is modelled by a rank-n correlation matrix. Instead, we use the formulation (5.18) in terms of orthogonal Brownian motions, but with the n forward rates driven by an m-dimensional rather than n-dimensional Brownian motion, with m much smaller than n.

5.9 Swap market model

Consider a unit notional amount and a set of dates $T_0 < T_1 < \cdots < T_n$ with accrual periods $\tau_i = T_i - T_{i-1}$ for $i = 1, \ldots, n$, and a forward interest rate swap (payer or receiver) at time $t < T_0$ with reset dates $T_0, \ldots, T_{n-1}$ and settlement dates $T_1, \ldots, T_n$.

Recall from Section 1.6 that the forward swap rate, denoted by $S_{0,n}(t)$, is the value of the fixed rate that makes the swap contract have zero value at time t. According to (1.15), it can be expressed as

$$S_{0,n}(t) = \frac{B(t, T_0) - B(t, T_n)}{A_{0,n}(t)}. \tag{5.31}$$

The denominator

$$A_{0,n}(t) = \sum_{k=1}^{n} \tau_k B(t, T_k) \tag{5.32}$$

in (5.31) is referred to as the **swap annuity** or **level**.

If we choose $A_{0,n}(t)$ as numeraire, the swap rate $S_{0,n}(t)$ discounted by $A_{0,n}(t)$ becomes a martingale under the associated measure P_A, called the the **forward swap measure** or simply the **swap measure**. This is because, according to (5.31), the swap rate $S_{0,n}(t)$ can be seen as the value $B(t, T_0) - B(t, T_n)$ of a portfolio of zero-coupon bonds discounted by the swap annuity $A_{0,n}(t)$.

In the **swap market model** (SMM) the forward swap rate $S_{0,n}(t)$ follows log-normal dynamics. Because $S_{0,n}(t)$ is a martingale under the swap measure P_A, this can be achieved by assuming that $S_{0,n}(t)$ satisfies the SDE

$$dS_{0,n}(t) = \sigma_{0,n}(t)S_{0,n}(t)dW^A(t), \tag{5.33}$$

where $\sigma_{0,n}(t)$ is a deterministic time-dependent volatility and $W^A(t)$ is a Brownian motion under P_A.

5.10 Black's formula for swaptions

In Section 5.2 we saw how the fact that each forward rate $F_i(t)$ can be modelled as a driftless log-normal process under the forward measure P_{T_i} leads to Black's formula for caplets. Analogously, Black's formula for swaptions arises naturally within the SMM.

By (1.14), (1.15) and (5.32), the value of a payer swap at time t is

$$\mathbf{PS}(t) = A_{0,n}(t)(S_{0,n}(t) - K).$$

Consider a payer swaption. The swaption payoff at time T_0 is

$$\mathbf{PSwpt}_{0,n}(T_0) = (\mathbf{PS}(T_0))^+ = A_{0,n}(T_0)(S_{0,n}(T_0) - K)^+.$$

It follows by Proposition 2.2 that the value at time $t \leq T_0$ of the payer swaption can be written as

$$\mathbf{PSwpt}_{0,n}(t) = A_{0,n}(t)\mathbb{E}_{P_A}\left((S_{0,n}(T_0) - K)^+ \big| \mathcal{F}_t\right).$$

We derive Black's formula for the swaption by computing this expectation.

Exercise 5.11 Show that

$$\mathbf{PSwpt}_{0,n}(t) = A_{0,n}(t)(S_{0,n}(t)N(d_+) - KN(d_-)),$$

where

$$d_\pm = \frac{\ln \frac{S_{0,n}(t)}{K} \pm \frac{1}{2} \int_t^{T_0} \sigma_{0,n}(s)^2 ds}{\sqrt{\int_t^{T_0} \sigma_{0,n}(s)^2 ds}}.$$

Setting

$$v_{0,n} = \sqrt{\frac{1}{T_0 - t} \int_t^{T_0} \sigma_{0,n}(s)^2 ds}, \tag{5.34}$$

we recover Black's formula (2.26) for swaptions with $v_{0,n}$ substituted for the volatility σ, that is, we have

$$\mathbf{PSwpt}_{0,n}(t) = \mathbf{PSwpt}_{0,n}^{\text{Black}}(t; v_{0,n}).$$

We can think of $v_{0,n}$ as the model-implied swaption volatility. The swaption price in the SMM will be consistent with the market price when $v_{0,n} = \hat{\sigma}_{0,n}^{\text{swpt}}$; see Section 2.9.

5.11 LMM versus SMM

In this section we compare the LMM and SMM and discover that they are incompatible with one another. The forward LIBOR rates $F_i(t)$ and the swap rate $S_{0,n}(t)$ cannot simultaneously satisfy the assumptions of these models.

Suppose that the forward rates $F_i(t)$ satisfy the SDE (5.12) of the LMM under the terminal measure P_{T_n}. Switching from the terminal measure P_{T_n} to the swap measure P_A, we can write the SDE for $F_i(t)$ as

$$dF_i(t) = \mu_i^A(t)F_i(t)dt + \sigma_i(t)F_i(t)dZ_i^A(t), \tag{5.35}$$

where $Z_i^A(t)$ for $i = 1, \ldots n$ are correlated Brownian motions under P_A such that

$$dZ_i^A(t)dZ_j^A(t) = \rho_{i,j}dt \tag{5.36}$$

for all $i, j = 1, \ldots, n$. We switch to the swap measure P_A because $S_{0,n}(t)$ is a martingale under P_A. Using this to compute the volatility $\sigma_{0,n}(t)$ of the swap rate will lead to the conclusion that $S_{0,n}(t)$ is not log-normally distributed in the LMM, contrary to the assumption underlying the SMM.

Exercise 5.12 Show that $F_i(t)$ satisfies the SDE (5.35) under the swap measure P_A and derive a formula for the drift $\mu_i^A(t)$.

Next we write the swap rate in terms of the forward rates as

$$S_{0,n}(t) = \frac{B(t, T_0) - B(t, T_n)}{\sum_{j=1}^n \tau_j B(t, T_j)} = \frac{1 - \prod_{i=1}^n (1 + \tau_i F_i(t))^{-1}}{\sum_{j=1}^n \tau_j \prod_{i=1}^j (1 + \tau_i F_i(t))^{-1}}.$$

By Itô's lemma,

$$dS_{0,n}(t) = \sum_{i=1}^n \frac{\partial S_{0,n}(t)}{\partial F_i} dF_i(t) + (\cdots) dt,$$

where for the sake of brevity we abuse the notation slightly, regarding $S_{0,n}(t)$ as a function of the forward rates. (Strictly speaking, we should write $S_{0,n}(F_1(t), \ldots, F_n(t))$ in place of $S_{0,n}(t)$.) We do not specify the terms with dt explicitly as they are not needed. Substituting for $dF_i(t)$ from (5.35), we obtain

$$dS_{0,n}(t) = \sum_{i=1}^n \frac{\partial S_{0,n}(t)}{\partial F_i} \sigma_i(t) F_i(t) dZ_i^A(t). \tag{5.37}$$

All the terms containing dt disappear because $S_{0,n}(t)$ is a martingale and the $Z_i^A(t)$ are Brownian motions under the swap measure P_A.

We are ready to compute the volatility $\sigma_{0,n}(t)$ of the swap rate $S_{0,n}(t)$. From (5.33) we have

$$\sigma_{0,n}(t)^2 dt = \frac{dS_{0,n}(t)}{S_{0,n}(t)} \frac{dS_{0,n}(t)}{S_{0,n}(t)}. \tag{5.38}$$

Substituting the right-hand side of (5.37) for $dS_{0,n}(t)$ and using (5.36), we get

$$\sigma_{0,n}(t)^2 dt = \frac{dS_{0,n}(t)}{S_{0,n}(t)} \frac{dS_{0,n}(t)}{S_{0,n}(t)}$$

$$= \frac{\sum_{i,j=1}^{n} \frac{\partial S_{0,n}(t)}{\partial F_i} \frac{\partial S_{0,n}(t)}{\partial F_j} \sigma_i(t)\sigma_j(t)F_i(t)F_j(t)\rho_{i,j}}{S_{0,n}(t)^2} dt.$$

In the LMM $\sigma_{0,n}(t)$ is clearly not a deterministic function, which shows that the swap rate $S_{0,n}(t)$ does not follow a log-normal process under P_A. This allows us to conclude that the LMM is incompatible with the SMM.

Remark 5.12

Although we have formally demonstrated that the swap rate $S_{0,n}(t)$ does not follow a log-normal process under P_A in the LMM, in many practical applications it turns out that $S_{0,n}(t)$ is approximately log-normally distributed, and the inconsistency between the LMM and SMM can often be ignored.

5.12 LMM approximation for swaption volatility

According to (5.34), the swap volatility $\sigma_{0,n}(s)$ in the SMM dynamics (5.33) enters Black's formula (2.26) for swaptions via an integral of $\sigma_{0,n}(s)^2$. We saw in Section 5.11 that, within the LMM, this integral is random. Nonetheless, we can approximate it by a deterministic quantity, making it possible to express Black's swaption volatility $\sigma_{0,n}(s)$ in the SMM via the parameters of the LMM. This simplifies calibration, when we often need to evaluate a wide range of swaptions quickly and accurately.

According to (1.16), we can express the swap rate as a linear combination of the forward rates $F_i(s) = F(s, T_{i-1}, T_i)$ for $i = 1, \ldots, n$, namely

$$S_{0,n}(s) = \sum_{i=1}^{n} w_i(s)F_i(s),$$

where the weights $w_i(s)$ are

$$w_i(s) = \frac{\tau_i B(s, T_i)}{A_{0,n}(s)}.$$

By Itô's lemma,

$$dS_{0,n}(s) = \sum_{i=1}^{n} w_i(s)dF_i(s) + \sum_{i=1}^{n} F_i(s)dw_i(s) + (\cdots)\,ds, \qquad (5.39)$$

where the terms with ds are not written explicitly as they will not be needed. Using (5.35), we get

$$dS_{0,n}(s) = \sum_{i=1}^{n} w_i(s)F_i(s)\sigma_i(s)dZ_i^A(s) + \sum_{i=1}^{n} F_i(s)dw_i(s).$$

All terms containing ds disappear on the right-hand side in the last expression because $S_{0,n}(s)$ is a martingale under the swap measure P_A, and so are $Z_i^A(s)$ and $w_i(s)$ for each $i = 1, \ldots, n$.

Since the weights $w_i(s)$ are martingales under P_A, it follows that the stochastic integrals $\int_t^s F_i(u)dw_i(u)$ are also martingales under P_A. In practice, their variability is often lower than that of $S_{0,n}(s)$. As the martingales do not vary much from their value at t, they can be approximated by this value, which is 0 and gives

$$dS_{0,n}(s) \approx \sum_{i=1}^{n} w_i(s)F_i(s)\sigma_i(s)dZ_i^A(s).$$

Consequently, substituting this into (5.38), we obtain

$$\sigma_{0,n}(s)^2 ds = \frac{dS_{0,n}(s)}{S_{0,n}(s)} \frac{dS_{0,n}(s)}{S_{0,n}(s)}$$
$$\approx \frac{\sum_{i,j=1}^{n} w_i(s)F_i(s)w_j(s)F_j(s)}{S_{0,n}(s)^2}\sigma_i(s)\sigma_j(s)\rho_{i,j}ds.$$

In the last expression there are more martingales under P_A, namely

$$S_{0,n}(s) = \frac{B(s,T_0) - B(s,T_n)}{A_{0,n}(s)}$$

and

$$w_i(s)F_i(s) = \frac{B(s,T_{i-1}) - B(s,T_i)}{A_{0,n}(s)}.$$

For any $s \in [t, T_0]$ these martingales can be approximated by their values at t, yielding

$$\sigma_{0,n}(s)^2 ds \approx \frac{\sum_{i,j=1}^{n} w_i(t)F_i(t)w_j(t)F_j(t)}{S_{0,n}(t)^2}\sigma_i(s)\sigma_j(s)\rho_{i,j}ds.$$

It follows that the volatility (5.34) in Black's swaption formula can be approximated as

$$
\begin{aligned}
v_{0,n}^2 &= \frac{1}{T_0 - t} \int_t^{T_0} \sigma_{0,n}(s)^2 ds \\
&\approx \frac{1}{T_0 - t} \sum_{i,j=1}^n \frac{w_i(t)w_j(t)F_i(t)F_j(t)}{S_{0,n}(t)^2} \int_t^{T_0} \sigma_i(s)\sigma_j(s)\rho_{i,j} ds.
\end{aligned} \tag{5.40}
$$

This approximation is known as **Rebonato's formula**. Without the means of approximating Black's swaption volatility $v_{0,n}$ and thus calculating the swaption price, calibration would become time consuming, which is why the approximation is important.

Remark 5.13

The accuracy of Rebonato's formula can be improved by approximating the martingale

$$
\int_t^s F_i(u)dw_i(u) = \sum_{j=1}^n \int_t^s F_i(u)\frac{\partial w_u(t)}{\partial F_j}F_j(u)\sigma_j(u)dZ_j^A(u)
$$

by

$$
\sum_{j=1}^n F_i(t)\frac{\partial w_i(t)}{\partial F_j}F_j(t)\int_t^s \sigma_j(u)dZ_j^A(u)
$$

rather than by its value at $s = t$, which is 0. (Here we consider the weights as functions of the forward rates, and strictly speaking should write $w_i(F_1(s), \ldots, F_n(s))$ in place of $w_i(s)$.)

6

Implementation and calibration of the LMM

In Chapter 5 we suggested possible parametric forms for both the instantaneous volatility and correlation. Here we use the functional form (5.25) for the instantaneous volatility. We also modelled the correlation between different forward rates by first deriving a sample correlation matrix (see Figure 5.4) based on historical data and then fitting this to a smooth parametric form so as to obtain a full-rank correlation matrix with the desired properties (Figure 5.5). In the present chapter we examine ways of taking this correlation matrix and producing a low-rank approximation convenient for numerical simulation.

In many applications the Monte Carlo method is the only feasible way to simulate the LMM dynamics. It is also the most general and readily applicable numerical method. For this reason, we discuss how to simulate the LMM dynamics in a Monte Carlo framework, starting with the popular Euler scheme, followed by the predictor-corrector method.

Another key issue is calibration. The model should reproduce the vanilla market. In other words, we need to calibrate the model parameters to the prices of traded swaptions and caps/floors. In effect, we use a stochastic interest rate model such as the LMM to infer the price of an exotic option from the market prices of vanilla instruments.

Since market prices are quoted as implied Black volatilities for a given maturity and strike, we also have to incorporate the volatility smile. To keep the presentation simple we do not discuss the volatility smile until Chapter 8.

6.1 Rank reduction

In a typical application of the LMM, for reasons of numerical efficiency, we seldom use the LMM formulation (5.2) whose correlation structure is modelled by a rank-n correlation matrix given by (5.1). Rather, we adopt an LMM formulation similar to (5.18), namely

$$dF_i(t) = \mu_i^j(t)F_i(t)dt + \sigma_i(t)F_i(t) \sum_{k=1}^{m} \eta_{i,k}dW_k^j(t),$$

but with the n forward rates driven by an m-dimensional Brownian motion $(W_1^j(t), \ldots, W_m^j(t))$, where $m < n$ (in fact sometimes $m \ll n$). The correlation matrix we use in this approach is a rank-m (rather than n) matrix given by

$$\rho_{i,j} = \sum_{k=1}^{m} \eta_{i,k}\eta_{j,k},$$

where $\eta = (\eta_{i,k})$ is an $n \times m$ matrix.

Denote by $\bar{\rho}$ an exogenously given correlation matrix of rank n, which we could take to be the sample correlation matrix in Figure 5.4, some smooth parametric form as in Figure 5.5 or another correlation structure. What we want is a rank-m correlation matrix ρ that approximates the exogenous full-rank matrix $\bar{\rho}$.

Spectral decomposition

One way of approximating the full-rank $n \times n$ correlation matrix $\bar{\rho}$ by a rank $m < n$ matrix ρ is to use spectral decomposition. Being a real symmetric $n \times n$ matrix, $\bar{\rho}$ can be represented as

$$\bar{\rho} = \bar{U}\bar{\Lambda}\bar{U}^\top,$$

where $\bar{U}$ is an orthonormal matrix whose columns are the eigenvectors of $\bar{\rho}$ and $\bar{\Lambda}$ is a diagonal matrix whose elements are the corresponding eigenvalues. The correlation matrix $\bar{\rho}$ is positive definite if and only if all the eigenvalues are positive. If all the eigenvalues are non-negative, the matrix is positive semidefinite. However, a correlation matrix derived using historical data such as the sample correlation matrix in Figure 5.4 may have some negative eigenvalues.

If the number of positive eigenvalues is greater than m, we can create a valid correlation matrix ρ of rank m as follows. Sort the eigenvalues in descending order $\lambda_1 \geq \cdots \geq \lambda_n$, and use the first m eigenvalues $\lambda_1 \geq \cdots \geq \lambda_m$ to form a new $m \times m$ diagonal matrix Λ and a new $n \times m$ matrix U whose columns are the eigenvectors corresponding to eigenvalue entries in Λ. Then an $n \times m$ matrix η can be defined as

$$\eta = DU\Lambda^{1/2},$$

where D is an $n \times n$ diagonal 'scaling' matrix chosen so that the row vectors of η have unit length. The diagonal entries of D are

$$d_i = \left(\sum_{k=1}^{m} U_{ik}^2 \lambda_k \right)^{-1/2}$$

for $i = 1, \ldots, n$. Finally, we put

$$\rho = \eta \eta^{\top},$$

which is a real symmetric positive definite matrix of rank m with unit diagonal entries.

Hypersphere decomposition

Another popular method for creating a low-rank correlation matrix is via **hypersphere decomposition**. In this method the row vectors of matrix η are given by points on the surface of a unit hypersphere in m dimensions in terms of angular coordinates. The elements of the $n \times m$ matrix η are expressed in terms of an $n \times (m-1)$ matrix of angular coordinates θ as

$$\eta_{i,j}(\theta) = \cos \theta_{i,j} \prod_{k=1}^{j-1} \sin \theta_{i,k}, \qquad 1 \leq j < m, \tag{6.1a}$$

$$\eta_{i,m}(\theta) = \prod_{k=1}^{m-1} \sin \theta_{i,k}, \tag{6.1b}$$

where we adopt the convention that $\prod_{k=1}^{0} \sin \theta_{i,k} = 1$. Then we put

$$\rho_{i,j}(\theta) = \sum_{k=1}^{m} \eta_{i,k}(\theta)\eta_{j,k}(\theta) \tag{6.2}$$

for each $i, j = 1, \ldots, n$, that is,

$$\rho(\theta) = \eta(\theta)\eta(\theta)^{\top}.$$

Example 6.1
In the case of a four-factor correlation structure, i.e. when four independent Brownian motions are used, the reduced-rank correlation structure based on angular coordinates is given by an $n \times 4$ matrix η whose ith row is

$$\left[\; \cos \theta_{i,1} \quad \sin \theta_{i,1} \cos \theta_{i,2} \quad \sin \theta_{i,1} \sin \theta_{i,2} \cos \theta_{i,3} \quad \sin \theta_{i,1} \sin \theta_{i,2} \sin \theta_{i,3} \; \right]$$

for $i = 1, \ldots, n$.

Exercise 6.1 Show that the Euclidean norm of each row of $\eta(\theta)$ is equal to 1, and therefore all the diagonal elements of $\rho(\theta)$ are equal to 1.

Exercise 6.2 Show that $\rho(\theta)$ is a positive semidefinite matrix.

We use numerical optimisation to calculate the angular parameters for a given exogenous correlation matrix $\bar{\rho}$:

$$\min_{\theta} \sum_{i,j=1}^{n} \left(\bar{\rho}_{i,j} - \rho_{i,j}(\theta) \right)^2. \tag{6.3}$$

Example 6.2
Taking the exogenous correlation matrix $\bar{\rho}$ to be the smooth parametric correlation matrix in Figure 5.5, we can perform the optimisation (6.3) to obtain a rank-4 correlation matrix $\rho(\theta)$ as shown in Figure 6.1.

Parameter reduction

When performing the optimisation (6.3), we are solving for $n(m-1)$ angular parameters, which could be more than the number $\frac{n(n-1)}{2}$ of parameters

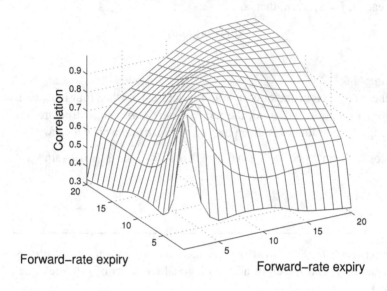

Figure 6.1 The rank-4 correlation matrix $\rho(\theta)$ after calibration to the correlation matrix in Figure 5.5.

needed to characterise the $n \times n$ correlation matrix, a symmetric matrix with all diagonal entries equal to 1. In particular, when $m = n$, the number of angular parameters is $n(n - 1)$, double that needed to characterise the correlation matrix.

We can utilise the rotational symmetry of the unit hypersphere in m dimensions to reduce the number of angular parameters. The entries of the correlation matrix ρ are determined by the scalar products of the unit vectors (i.e. points on the hypersphere) corresponding to the rows of the matrix η. Rotations of the hypersphere do not alter these scalar products, which makes it possible to fix some of the angular parameters.

Namely, rotating the hypersphere allows us to align the first row in η with the unit vector

$$(1, 0, \ldots, 0) \in \mathbb{R}^m,$$

which corresponds to setting

$$\theta_{1,1} = \theta_{1,2} = \cdots = \theta_{1,m-1} = 0.$$

While keeping the first row fixed, we can rotate the hypersphere once again to align the second row of η with the unit vector

$$(\cos \theta_{2,1}, \sin \theta_{2,1}, 0, \ldots, 0) \in \mathbb{R}^m.$$

This corresponds to setting

$$\theta_{2,2} = \cdots = \theta_{2,m-1} = 0.$$

The rotational symmetry of the hypersphere allows us to proceed in this manner up to and including the $(m-1)$st row in η, setting

$$\theta_{1,1} = \theta_{1,2} = \cdots = \theta_{1,m-1} = 0,$$
$$\theta_{2,2} = \cdots = \theta_{2,m-1} = 0,$$
$$\vdots$$
$$\theta_{m-1,m-1} = 0.$$

This reduces the number of angular parameters by $\frac{m(m-1)}{2}$.

Exercise 6.3 Show that the number of angular parameters remaining after the reduction does not exceed the number of parameters characterising the $n \times n$ correlation matrix, that is,

$$n(m-1) - \frac{m(m-1)}{2} \le \frac{n(n-1)}{2}$$

for any $m \le n$.

Example 6.3
When $m = 4$ (four independent Brownian motions), the matrix $\eta(\theta)$ is given by

$$\begin{bmatrix} 1 & 0 & 0 & 0 \\ \cos \theta_{2,1} & \sin \theta_{2,1} & 0 & 0 \\ \cos \theta_{3,1} & \cos \theta_{3,2} \sin \theta_{3,1} & \sin \theta_{3,1} \sin \theta_{3,2} & 0 \\ \cos \theta_{4,1} & \cos \theta_{4,2} \sin \theta_{4,1} & \cos \theta_{4,3} \sin \theta_{4,1} \sin \theta_{4,2} & \sin \theta_{4,1} \sin \theta_{4,2} \sin \theta_{4,3} \\ \vdots & \vdots & \vdots & \vdots \\ \cos \theta_{n,1} & \cos \theta_{n,2} \sin \theta_{n,1} & \cos \theta_{n,3} \sin \theta_{n,1} \sin \theta_{n,2} & \sin \theta_{n,1} \sin \theta_{n,2} \sin \theta_{n,3} \end{bmatrix}$$

Therefore we need to solve for $3(n-2)$ unknowns in the above as opposed to $3n$ unknowns in the original parameterisation.

6.2 Monte Carlo simulation

Consider a European derivative security with expiry date T_j and payoff of
the form $h(F_1(T_j), \ldots, F_n(T_j))$ that depends on the forward rates $F_i(T_j) =$
$F(T_j; T_{i-1}, T_i)$ for $i = j + 1, \ldots, n$ as well as on the LIBOR rates that will
have set by time T_j and are denoted here by $F_i(T_j) = L(T_{i-1}, T_i)$ for $i =$
$1, \ldots, j$. The price at time 0 of this option can be expressed as

$$B(0, T_n) \mathbb{E}_{P_{T_n}} \left(\frac{h(F_1(T_j), \ldots, F_n(T_j))}{B(T_j, T_n)} \right),$$

where we take the bond $B(t, T_n)$ as numeraire and write the option price in
terms of the expectation with respect to the terminal measure P_{T_n}.

We want to compute this expectation by using the LMM dynamics of
the forward rates under the chosen measure. However, since the LMM dynamics does not give rise to a known distribution, we need to employ some
form of numerical approximation. Given the large number of state variables, we will be better off using Monte Carlo simulation rather than finite
difference techniques.

To evaluate the expected payoff of an option via Monte Carlo simulation
we simulate the evolution through time (called a path) of the set of spanning
forward rates $F_1(t), F_2(t), \ldots, F_n(t)$ and compute the payoff discounted by
the numeraire. Repeating the simulation, we compute the discounted payoff
values for several different paths. Finally, we calculate the mean of these
discounted payoffs to obtain an estimate of the expected payoff.

There are a number of ways of evolving the entire forward LIBOR curve
through time that are consistent with the model dynamics. We assume the
LMM dynamics is formulated in terms of a set of $m \le n$ orthogonal Brownian motions, see Section 6.1. With the T_n-bond $B(t, T_n)$ chosen as numeraire, the dynamics of the forward rates is given as

$$dF_i(t) = \mu_i^n(F(t), t) F_i(t) dt + \sigma_i(t) F_i(t) \sum_{k=1}^{m} \eta_{i,k} dW_k^n(t), \qquad (6.4)$$

where the $\sigma_i(t)$ are the instantaneous volatilities and the instantaneous correlations are

$$\rho_{i,j} = \sum_{k=1}^{m} \eta_{i,k} \eta_{j,k},$$

and where we make the dependence of the drift on the vector $F(t) =$
$(F_1(t), \ldots, F_n(t))$ of forward rates explicit. By (5.13), the drift can be ex-

pressed as

$$\mu_i^n(F(t), t) = -\sum_{k=i+1}^{n} \frac{\tau_k \rho_{k,i} \sigma_i(t) \sigma_k(t) F_k(t)}{1 + \tau_k F_k(t)} \tag{6.5}$$

for any $t \in [0, T_{i-1}]$.

The simplest time-stepping procedure is the **Euler scheme**. Given numerically estimated forward rates $\bar{F}_i(t)$ at time t, we can estimate the rates at time $t + \Delta t$ as

$$\bar{F}_i(t + \Delta t) = \bar{F}_i(t) + \mu_i^n(\bar{F}(t), t)\Delta t + \sigma_i(t) \sqrt{\Delta t} \sum_{k=1}^{m} \eta_{i,k} \varepsilon_k,$$

where $\varepsilon_1, \ldots, \varepsilon_m$ is a vector of m independent random variables, each following the standard normal distribution $N(0, 1)$. The step size Δt is often taken to be the forward-rate accrual period, with the simulation times chosen to match the setting dates $T_0, \ldots, T_{n-1}$ of the forward LIBOR rates.

Remark 6.4

A particular drawback with the Euler scheme is its slow rate of convergence. We can improve convergence by working with the logarithms of the forward LIBOR rates rather than the rates themselves. Applying Itô's formula to the LMM dynamics, we have

$$d(\ln F_i(t)) = \left(\mu_i^n(F(t), t) - \frac{1}{2}\sigma_i(t)^2\right)dt + \sigma_i(t) \sum_{k=1}^{m} \eta_{i,k} dW_k^n(t).$$

This leads to the Euler scheme

$$\ln \bar{F}_i(t + \Delta t) = \ln \bar{F}_i(t) + \left(\mu_i^n(\bar{F}(t), t) - \frac{1}{2}\sigma_i(t)^2\right)\Delta t + \sigma_i(t) \sqrt{\Delta t} \sum_{k=1}^{m} \eta_{i,k} \varepsilon_k, \tag{6.6}$$

where $\varepsilon_1, \ldots, \varepsilon_m$ are as above.

Predictor-corrector method

A popular way of improving the Euler scheme is to apply a **predictor-corrector method**. Given predictor-corrector estimates $\bar{F}_i(t)$ of the rates at time t, we first calculate estimates $\tilde{F}_i(t + \Delta t)$ of the forward LIBOR rates at time $t + \Delta t$ by using the Euler scheme, namely

$$\ln \tilde{F}_i(t + \Delta t) = \ln \bar{F}_i(t) + \left(\mu_i^n(\bar{F}(t), t) - \frac{1}{2}\sigma_i(t)^2\right)\Delta t + \sigma_i(t) \sqrt{\Delta t} \sum_{k=1}^{m} \eta_{i,k} \varepsilon_k.$$

We then recompute the drift term by using the estimated LIBOR rates $\tilde{F}_i(t+\Delta t)$, that is, evaluate $\mu_i^n(\tilde{F}(t+\Delta t), t+\Delta t)$. Finally, we re-estimate the forward LIBOR rates using the same vector of standard normals $\varepsilon_1, \ldots, \varepsilon_m$, but with a new 'predictor-corrector' drift. This can be written as

$$\ln \bar{F}_i(t + \Delta t) = \ln \bar{F}_i(t)$$

$$+ \left(\theta \mu_i^n(\bar{F}(t), t) + (1 - \theta)\mu_i^n(\tilde{F}(t + \Delta t), t + \Delta t) - \frac{1}{2}\sigma_i(t)^2 \right) \Delta t$$

$$+ \sigma_i(t) \sqrt{\Delta t} \sum_{k=1}^{m} \eta_{i,k}\varepsilon_k,$$

where $\theta \in [0, 1]$.

For $\theta = 1$ the scheme is said to be fully explicit. In this case it is identical to the simple Euler scheme. For $\theta = 0$ the scheme is fully implicit. Market practitioners typically choose $\theta = 0.5$.

Remark 6.5

A well-known weakness of Monte Carlo simulation is its slow rate of convergence. For N simulated paths the error is proportional to $1/\sqrt{N}$. This means that to get an accurate estimate of the option price we need to perform a prohibitively large number of simulations. Fortunately, there are several so-called variance-reduction techniques that can be applied to improve convergence. Examples are the control variate technique and the antithetic variable technique. Error reduction via a control variate is covered in [NMFC].

Monte Carlo pricing of Bermudan swaptions

Above we discussed Monte Carlo simulation as applied to pricing interest rate derivatives of European type. However, the method is just as useful for pricing other exotic derivatives. The Bermudan swaption, which was discussed in Section 3.6, is a good example of the type of instrument for which Monte Carlo simulation is often the only viable numerical approach when we are working in the LMM framework.

We recall that, for a set of dates $0 < T_0 < T_1 < \cdots < T_n$, the holder of a payer (or receiver) Bermudan swaption with strike K has the right to enter a payer (or receiver) interest rate swap with swap rate K at any time T_k, where $k = 0, \ldots, l$. The value of the option at time T_i is given by (3.30), that is, it is the maximum of the exercise value $E(T_i)$ and the continuation value $C(T_i)$.

In Section 3.6 the value of the Bermudan at time 0 was found recursively, starting at the last exercise date and working backwards in time. The difficulty is that, in a Monte Carlo simulation, the paths of the underlying forward LIBOR rates are generated forward in time, so at time T_i the future values of the rates $F_j(t)$ with $j > i + 1$ remain unknown. As a consequence, the continuation value $C(T_i)$ is also unknown. This makes it difficult to apply (3.30).

One way of overcoming this difficulty is to use an approximation to the continuation value. A popular approach is the method of Longstaff and Schwartz, where an approximation is found by regressing estimates of the continuation value on an appropriate set of basis functions. However, the details of this important application of the Monte Carlo method are beyond the scope of this book.

6.3 Calibration

There are several different (though closely related) approaches we can take when it comes to calibrating the model parameters. The deciding factor in choosing one method over another will depend on the derivative we need to value.

Calibrating to caplets

The following procedure is suitable for instruments whose price depends mainly on caplet volatility. We use the time-homogeneous parametric form (5.25) for the instantaneous volatility, which we write as

$$\sigma_i(t; \alpha) = (a + b(T_{i-1} - t))e^{-c(T_{i-1}-t)} + d,$$

with α denoting the set of parameters a, b, c, d. As shown in Section 5.2, the time 0 price of the ith caplet in the LMM is given by Black's formula (2.24) with

$$v_i(\alpha) = \sqrt{\frac{1}{T_{i-1}} \int_0^{T_{i-1}} \sigma_i(t; \alpha)^2 dt}$$

substituted for the volatility σ. Taking the volatilities $\hat{\sigma}_i^{\text{caplet}}$ implied by the market prices of caplets via (2.25), we can perform the least squares optimisation

$$\min_{\alpha} \sum_{i=1}^{n} \left((\hat{\sigma}_i^{\text{caplet}})^2 - v_i(\alpha)^2 \right)^2 \tag{6.7}$$

to calibrate the parameters.

With just four parameters, the time-homogeneous form (5.25) for the instantaneous volatility may not be flexible enough to provide a good fit to the observed data. To obtain a perfect fit we can introduce a constant parameter κ_i for each forward LIBOR rate $F_i(t)$ and write the instantaneous volatility as

$$\sigma_i(t) = \kappa_i \sigma_i(t; \alpha). \tag{6.8}$$

Since the parameters κ_i are unique to each forward LIBOR rate, this new form for the instantaneous volatility is no longer time homogeneous. To calibrate to the set of observed caplet volatilities we can use the parameters α found by the least squares optimisation (6.7) and choose the κ_i so that

$$\hat{\sigma}_i^{\text{caplet}} = \kappa_i v_i(\alpha). \tag{6.9}$$

In practice this gives values of κ_i that are typically close to 1, so we can think of (6.8) as approximately time homogeneous.

Calibrating to swaptions

In general, we need to calibrate to the implied swaption volatilities in addition to implied caplet volatilities. For example, when valuing a Bermudan swaption we should aim for the exact recovery of the set of co-terminal swaptions that underlie the Bermudan.

Since calibrating to a large matrix of swaption prices (equivalently, implied Black swaption volatilities) is computationally intensive, the standard approach is to use an analytic approximation to Black's swaption volatility, which makes it possible to quickly calculate the volatility given a set of model parameters. A popular analytic approximation for Black's swaption volatility is Rebonato's formula (5.40). To adapt the formula for a T_l into $T_m - T_l$ swaption, we need to replace the indices $0, n$ by l, m. This gives the following approximation for the volatility (5.34) in Black's formula for such a swaption:

$$v_{l,m}^2 = \frac{1}{T_l} \sum_{i,j=l+1}^{m} \frac{w_i(0) w_j(0) F_i(0) F_j(0)}{S_{l,m}(0)^2} \int_0^{T_l} \sigma_i(t) \sigma_j(t) \rho_{i,j} dt, \tag{6.10}$$

where

$$w_i(t) = \frac{\tau_i B(t, T_i)}{\displaystyle\sum_{j=l+1}^{m} \tau_j B(t, T_j)} = \frac{\displaystyle\tau_i \prod_{k=l+1}^{i} \frac{1}{1 + \tau_k F_k(t)}}{\displaystyle\sum_{j=l+1}^{m} \tau_j \prod_{k=l+1}^{j} \frac{1}{1 + \tau_k F_k(t)}}.$$

Having chosen the functional form (6.8) for the instantaneous volatility, and (6.1) and (6.2) with parameter reduction for the instantaneous correlation, we denote the model parameters κ_i, $i = 1, \ldots, n$ and a, b, c, d for the volatility by κ and α, and those for the correlation by θ. Thus the volatility in Black's swaption formula approximated by using (6.10) can be denoted by $v_{l,m}(\kappa, \alpha, \theta)$.

One approach to calibration would be to take the market-implied swaption volatilities $\hat{\sigma}_{l,m}^{\text{swpt}}$ and the corresponding Black swaption volatilities $v_{l,m}(\kappa, \alpha, \theta)$ calculated by using (6.10), and to perform the least squares optimisation

$$\min_{\kappa, \alpha, \theta} \sum_{l,m} a_{l,m} \left((\hat{\sigma}_{l,m}^{\text{swpt}})^2 - v_{l,m}(\kappa, \alpha, \theta)^2 \right)^2 \tag{6.11}$$

with some weights $a_{l,m}$. The choice of these weights depends on the instrument to be valued. In particular, for a Bermudan swaption we need to recover as accurately as possible the implied volatilities of the co-terminal swaptions, therefore we could make the weights associated with the co-terminal set equal to 1 and all the remaining weights equal to 0.

A major drawback of the above optimisation is that fitting the correlation parameters to the implied volatilities by means of (6.11) will often result in a 'noisy' correlation structure with features that contradict those observed empirically. The implied Black volatility is only weakly dependent on the instantaneous correlation. This makes it difficult to infer the 'correct' correlation structure from the implied volatilities. For this reason, practitioners will often estimate the correlation parameters from a sample correlation matrix calculated using historical data, such as the one in Figure 5.4. This approach is outlined in Section 5.8. As a result, we can drop θ in the optimisation problem (6.11) and calibrate only to the instantaneous volatility parameters κ and α. Moreover, we can also drop κ by defining the κ_i by means of (6.9) as functions of the parameters $\alpha = (a, b, c, d)$, thereby achieving a perfect fit to the caplet volatilities $\hat{\sigma}_i^{\text{caplet}}$ given by the market.

In general, the chosen parameterisation may not be rich enough to ensure an accurate fit to all caplets and the entire swaption matrix. As is often the case for calibration problems, we need to make a compromise between the accuracy of the fit and ensuring that the behaviour of the model as implied by the choice of parameters is realistic.

6.4 Numerical example

We present an example of European option pricing via Monte Carlo simulation. Consider a set of dates $0 = T_0 < T_1 < \cdots < T_n$ with accrual periods $\tau_i = T_i - T_{i-1}$ for $i = 1, \ldots, n$, and suppose that the initial term structure of forward LIBOR rates $F_i(T_0)$ for $i = 1, \ldots, n$ is given along with the implied Black caplet volatilities $\hat{\sigma}_i^{\text{caplet}}$ for $i = 2, \ldots, n$. Note that the first forward rate $F_1(T_0) = L(T_0, T_1)$ will have set at time T_0, therefore we shall be simulating the evolution in time of a set of $n - 1$ forward rates. For simplicity we consider the one-factor case, with $m = 1$ in (6.4).

To begin, we need to calibrate the instantaneous volatility $\sigma_i(t)$ to the implied volatilities $\hat{\sigma}_i^{\text{caplet}}$. We assume the time-homogeneous piecewise constant form (5.24) for the instantaneous volatility, which allows us to apply a bootstrapping method rather than the more involved least squares optimisation (6.7). For each $i = 2, \ldots, n$ the implied volatility $\hat{\sigma}_i^{\text{caplet}}$ quoted in the market is set equal to the LMM implied volatility (5.9), namely

$$\left(\hat{\sigma}_i^{\text{caplet}}\right)^2 = v_i^2 = \frac{1}{T_{i-1}} \int_0^{T_{i-1}} \sigma_i(s)^2 ds = \frac{1}{T_{i-1}} \sum_{j=1}^{i-1} \sigma_{i-j}^2 (T_j - T_{j-1}).$$

In particular, $\sigma_1 = \hat{\sigma}_2^{\text{caplet}}$. Moreover, if we have already computed the piecewise constant volatilities $\sigma_1, \ldots, \sigma_{i-2}$ for some i, then we can obtain σ_{i-1} by rewriting the above as

$$\sigma_{i-1}^2 = \frac{1}{T_1} \left(T_{i-1} \left(\hat{\sigma}_i^{\text{caplet}}\right)^2 - \sum_{j=2}^{i-1} \sigma_{i-j}^2 (T_j - T_{j-1}) \right).$$

Example 6.6
The initial term structure of forward LIBOR rates $F_i(T_0)$ for $i = 1, \ldots, n$ is given in Table 6.1 along with the implied Black caplet volatilities $\hat{\sigma}_i^{\text{caplet}}$ for $i = 2, \ldots, n$, with $n = 12$ and accrual periods $\tau_i = T_i - T_{i-1} = 0.25$ years for $i = 1, \ldots, n$. Calibrating as above to the implied volatilities $\hat{\sigma}_i^{\text{caplet}}$, we

Table 6.1 *Quarterly forward LIBOR rates $F_i(T_0)$ and implied caplet volatilities $\hat{\sigma}_i^{\text{caplet}}$ at time $T_0 = 0$.*

i	τ_i	$F_i(T_0)$	$\hat{\sigma}_i^{\text{caplet}}$
1	0.25	2.000%	
2	0.25	2.051%	40.000%
3	0.25	2.103%	39.012%
4	0.25	2.156%	38.049%
5	0.25	2.210%	37.110%
6	0.25	2.266%	36.193%
7	0.25	2.324%	35.300%
8	0.25	2.382%	34.428%
9	0.25	2.443%	33.578%
10	0.25	2.505%	32.749%
11	0.25	2.568%	31.941%
12	0.25	2.633%	31.152%

compute the piecewise constant volatilities σ_{i-1} for $i = 2, \ldots, 12$ listed in Table 6.2.

Once the model is calibrated, we are ready to evolve the set of forward rates though time. We use the Euler scheme (6.6) with time steps equal to the forward-rate accrual periods. Given the estimated forward rates $\bar{F}_i(T_j)$ at time T_j for some $j = 0, \ldots, n - 2$, we estimate the rates at time T_{j+1} as

$$\bar{F}_i(T_{j+1}) = \bar{F}_i(T_j) \exp\left(\left(\mu_i^n(\bar{F}(T_j), T_j) - \frac{1}{2}\sigma_i(T_j)^2\right)\tau_{j+1} + \sigma_i(T_j)\sqrt{\tau_{j+1}}\varepsilon\right)$$

for $i = j + 2, \ldots, n$, where ε is a random variable with the standard normal distribution $N(0, 1)$ and where the drift term is given by (6.5), which becomes

$$\mu_i^n(\bar{F}(T_j), T_j) = -\sum_{k=i+1}^{n} \frac{\tau_k \rho_{k,i} \sigma_i(T_j)\sigma_k(T_j)F_k(T_j)}{1 + \tau_k F_k(T_j)}.$$

Having estimated the forward rates at time T_j, we can compute the value at time T_j of the zero-coupon bond maturing at time T_i for $i = j + 1, \ldots, n$ as

$$B(T_j, T_i) = \prod_{k=j+1}^{i} \frac{1}{(1 + \tau_k \bar{F}_k(T_j))}.$$

Table 6.2 *Piecewise constant volatilities σ_{i-1} and LMM drift terms $\mu_i^n(\bar{F}(0), 0)$ used in the time T_1 estimate of the forward rate $\bar{F}_i(T_1)$. The zero-coupon bond prices $B(T_1, T_i)$ are also given.*

i	σ_{i-1}	$\mu_i^n(\bar{F}(0), 0)$	$\bar{F}_i(T_1)$	$B(T_1, T_i)$
2	40.000%	0.006 873	2.494%	0.993 80
3	37.999%	0.005 774	2.535%	0.987 54
4	36.046%	0.004 781	2.577%	0.981 22
5	34.137%	0.003 887	2.620%	0.974 84
6	32.269%	0.003 088	2.664%	0.968 39
7	30.441%	0.002 378	2.709%	0.961 87
8	28.647%	0.001 752	2.754%	0.955 30
9	26.886%	0.001 205	2.801%	0.948 65
10	25.152%	0.000 734	2.849%	0.941 95
11	23.440%	0.000 333	2.897%	0.935 17
12	21.746%	0.000 000	2.946%	0.928 34

Example 6.7

Continuing the numerical example, in Table 6.3 we show the evolution in time of the forward rates for a single simulated path. To keep the table concise, we list only the rates computed up to time T_6. In Table 6.2 we show the discount bonds $B(T_1, T_i)$, together with the drift terms $\mu_i^n(\bar{F}(0), 0)$, for the path whose fragment up to time T_6 is shown in Table 6.3.

For a derivative security that makes a payment $h(F_1(T_j), \ldots, F_n(T_j))$ at time T_j depending on the forward rates $F_i(T_j) = F(T_j; T_{i-1}, T_i)$ for $i = j + 1, \ldots, n$ as well as on the LIBOR rates $F_i(T_j) = L(T_{i-1}, T_i)$ for $i = 1, \ldots, j$ (a simple example being a caplet payment with payoff $(T_j - T_{j-1})(L(T_{j-1}, T_j) - K)^+$ at time T_j), the numeraire-discounted payoff expressed as a function of the Monte Carlo estimated rates $\bar{F}_1(T_j), \ldots, \bar{F}_n(T_j)$ is

$$\frac{h(\bar{F}_1(T_j), \ldots, \bar{F}_n(T_j))}{B(T_j, T_n)}.$$

We can compute the discounted payoff for a number of different paths by repeating the above simulation and then calculate the mean and multiply it by $B(0, T_n)$ to obtain a Monte Carlo estimate of the value of the derivative security at time $T_0 = 0$.

Table 6.3 *Estimated forward rates* $\bar{F}_i(t)$ *for* $t = T_0 \ldots, T_6$ *along a simulated path.*

t	T_0	T_1	T_2	T_3	T_4	T_5	T_6
ε		1.087 40	−1.166 18	0.213 40	−0.990 00	0.885 75	−2.022 10
$\bar{F}_1(t)$	2.000%						
$\bar{F}_2(t)$	2.051%	2.494%					
$\bar{F}_3(t)$	2.103%	2.535%	1.964%				
$\bar{F}_4(t)$	2.156%	2.577%	2.025%	2.068%			
$\bar{F}_5(t)$	2.210%	2.620%	2.087%	2.132%	1.712%		
$\bar{F}_6(t)$	2.266%	2.664%	2.149%	2.196%	1.785%	2.086%	
$\bar{F}_7(t)$	2.324%	2.709%	2.213%	2.261%	1.859%	2.159%	1.411%
$\bar{F}_8(t)$	2.382%	2.754%	2.279%	2.327%	1.935%	2.232%	1.492%
$\bar{F}_9(t)$	2.443%	2.801%	2.345%	2.394%	2.013%	2.307%	1.576%
$\bar{F}_{10}(t)$	2.505%	2.849%	2.413%	2.462%	2.092%	2.382%	1.662%
$\bar{F}_{11}(t)$	2.568%	2.897%	2.482%	2.531%	2.174%	2.458%	1.751%
$\bar{F}_{12}(t)$	2.633%	2.946%	2.552%	2.601%	2.256%	2.535%	1.842%

Example 6.8

Consider a cap with payment dates $T_2, \ldots, T_n$, a 1 million USD notional and strike of 1.75%. This simple example is a good test of Monte Carlo simulation in the LMM. We should be able to price caps very well given that the model has been calibrated to the implied caplet volatilities. Monte Carlo simulation with 100 000 paths does indeed produce a price within 0.05% of that given by Black's formula, which is $18 358.

In Section 7.4 we are going to use the same approach to price a ratchet floater.

7

Valuing interest rate derivatives

In this chapter we study a number of examples of interest rate derivatives, which can be valued by a variety of methods. Categorising the range of different instruments traded in the market is a difficult task. Indeed there is no universally agreed taxonomy. We are going to describe a subset of the payoffs encountered in the market.

Derivatives such as in-arrears swaps and constant-maturity swaps (CMS) can be valued by applying what is known as a convexity correction or adjustment to the underlying interest rate. This convexity adjustment arises in cases when we take the expected value of an interest rate, for example the forward LIBOR rate $F_i(t) = F(t; T_{i-1}, T_i)$ or the forward swap rate $S_{0,n}(t)$, under a probability measure other than that which makes the rate a martingale, i.e. other than the forward measure P_{T_i} for $F_i(t)$ or the forward swap measure P_A for $S_{0,n}(t)$. In this way we can obtain an analytic formula or approximation for these instruments.

For some derivatives an accurate analytic formula or approximation may not be available, and a numerical method needs to be deployed such as Monte Carlo simulation. As examples of such derivatives we discuss ratchet floaters, range accruals and trigger swaps.

7.1 LIBOR-in-arrears

The simplest example of a convexity adjustment is the LIBOR-in-arrears payment. Consider a unit notional amount and a set of dates $0 \leq T_0 < T_1 < \cdots < T_n$ with accrual periods $\tau_i = T_i - T_{i-1}$ for $i = 1, \ldots, n$. The LIBOR rate

$$L(T_{i-1}, T_i) = \frac{1 - B(T_{i-1}, T_i)}{\tau_i B(T_{i-1}, T_i)}$$

is fixed at time T_{i-1} and pays an amount $\tau_i L(T_{i-1}, T_i)$ at time T_i. Denoting this amount at time T_i by

$$\mathbf{L}_i(T_i) = \tau_i L(T_{i-1}, T_i),$$

we can express its value at time 0 as

$$\mathbf{L}_i(0) = \tau_i B(0, T_i) \mathbb{E}_{P_{T_i}}(L(T_{i-1}, T_i)) = \tau_i B(0, T_i) F_i(0), \qquad (7.1)$$

where we use the T_i-bond as numeraire, compute the expectation under the corresponding forward measure P_{T_i} and use the fact that the forward rate

$$F_i(t) = F(t; T_{i-1}, T_i) = \frac{B(t, T_{i-1}) - B(t, T_i)}{\tau_i B(t, T_i)}$$

is a martingale under this measure, with $F_i(T_{i-1}) = L(T_{i-1}, T_i)$; see Section 2.4. Substituting this formula for the forward rate, we get the expression

$$\mathbf{L}_i(0) = B(0, T_{i-1}) - B(0, T_i).$$

The same result can be derived using a replication argument; see Proposition 1.4.

A **LIBOR-in-arrears** payment is based on the same rate $L(T_{i-1}, T_i)$, but the amount $\tau_i L(T_{i-1}, T_i)$ is paid at time T_{i-1} rather than T_i, that is, at the beginning rather than at the end of the accrual period. We denote this payment at time T_{i-1} by

$$\mathbf{Lia}_i(T_{i-1}) = \tau_i L(T_{i-1}, T_i).$$

The value at time 0 of the LIBOR-in-arrears payment can be expressed as

$$\mathbf{Lia}_i(0) = \tau_i B(0, T_{i-1}) \mathbb{E}_{P_{T_{i-1}}}(L(T_{i-1}, T_i)),$$

where we use the T_{i-1}-bond as numeraire and compute the expectation under the corresponding forward measure $P_{T_{i-1}}$.

However, we cannot evaluate the expectation $\mathbb{E}_{P_{T_{i-1}}}(L(T_{i-1}, T_i))$ as easily as $\mathbb{E}_{P_{T_i}}(L(T_{i-1}, T_i))$ because the forward rate $F_i(t)$ is not a martingale under $P_{T_{i-1}}$. To obtain an expression for $\mathbf{Lia}_i(0)$ similar to (7.1) we can perform a change of measure from $P_{T_{i-1}}$ to P_{T_i}. The Radon–Nikodym derivative of $P_{T_{i-1}}$ with respect to P_{T_i} is

$$\frac{dP_{T_{i-1}}}{dP_{T_i}} = \frac{B(0, T_i)}{B(0, T_{i-1})} \frac{1}{B(T_{i-1}, T_i)} = \frac{B(0, T_i)}{B(0, T_{i-1})} (1 + \tau_i L(T_{i-1}, T_i)).$$

It follows that

$$
\begin{aligned}
\mathbf{Lia}_i(0) &= \tau_i B(0, T_{i-1}) \mathbb{E}_{P_{T_{i-1}}} (L(T_{i-1}, T_i)) \\
&= \tau_i B(0, T_i) \mathbb{E}_{P_{T_i}} (L(T_{i-1}, T_i) (1 + \tau_i L(T_{i-1}, T_i))) \\
&= \tau_i B(0, T_i) \left(F_i(0) + \tau_i \mathbb{E}_{P_{T_i}} \left(L(T_{i-1}, T_i)^2 \right) \right) \\
&= \mathbf{L}_i(0) + \tau_i^2 B(0, T_i) \mathbb{E}_{P_{T_i}} \left(L(T_{i-1}, T_i)^2 \right).
\end{aligned}
$$

The term $\tau_i \mathbb{E}_{P_{T_i}} \left(L(T_{i-1}, T_i)^2 \right)$ is called the **convexity correction** or **convexity adjustment** to the forward rate $F_i(0)$.

Exercise 7.1   The **convexity-corrected** or **convexity-adjusted** forward rate $\bar{F}_i(t)$ is defined as

$$\bar{F}_i(t) = F_i(t) + \tau_i \mathbb{E}_{P_{T_i}} \left(L(T_{i-1}, T_i)^2 \big| \mathcal{F}_t \right)$$

for any $t \in [0, T_{i-1}]$. Show that $\bar{F}_i(t)$ is a martingale under P_{T_i} and that the value at time t of the LIBOR-in-arrears payment is

$$\mathbf{Lia}_i(t) = \tau_i B(t, T_i) \bar{F}_i(t).$$

We present two ways of evaluating the convexity correction. The first method uses replication by a portfolio of caplets, while the other assumes that the forward rate $F_i(t)$ satisfies the SDE (5.3) of the LMM, i.e. $F_i(t)$ is a driftless log-normal process with deterministic volatility $\sigma_i(t)$ under the forward measure P_{T_i}.

Portfolio replication

We begin by writing the square of the spot LIBOR rate as

$$L(T_{i-1}, T_i)^2 = 2 \int_0^\infty (L(T_{i-1}, T_i) - K)^+ \, dK.$$

Substituting this into the expression for $\mathbf{Lia}_i(0)$ gives

$$\mathbf{Lia}_i(0) = \mathbf{L}_i(0) + \tau_i^2 B(0, T_i) \mathbb{E}_{P_{T_i}} \left(L(T_{i-1}, T_i)^2 \right)$$

$$= \mathbf{L}_i(0) + 2\tau_i \int_0^\infty \tau_i B(0, T_i) \mathbb{E}_{P_{T_i}} ((L(T_{i-1}, T_i) - K)^+) \, dK$$

$$= \mathbf{L}_i(0) + 2\tau_i \int_0^\infty \mathbf{Cpl}_i(0, K) dK, \tag{7.2}$$

where we write $\mathbf{Cpl}_i(0, K)$ for the time-0 price of the ith caplet with strike rate K.

In reality the integral would be replaced by a discrete sum. In this way we express the value of the LIBOR-in-arrears in terms of the market prices of vanilla caplets at various strikes. This method has the advantage that it implicitly incorporates the interest rate smile (see Chapter 8 for a discussion of the interest rate smile). This is an accurate method of valuation, but can be computationally expensive.

Analytic expression in the LMM

Within the LMM framework the forward rate $F_i(t)$ is a driftless log-normal process under the forward measure P_{T_i}, which satisfies the SDE

$$dF_i(t) = \sigma_i(t) F_i(t) dZ_i^i(t)$$

with deterministic volatility $\sigma_i(t)$, where $Z_i^i(t)$ is a Brownian motion under P_{T_i}; see (5.3). As a result,

$$\mathbb{E}_{P_{T_i}} \left(L(T_{i-1}, T_i)^2 \right) = F_i(0)^2 e^{v_i^2 T_{i-1}}, \tag{7.3}$$

where

$$v_i = \sqrt{\frac{1}{T_{i-1}} \int_0^{T_{i-1}} \sigma_i(s)^2 ds}$$

is the caplet implied volatility (5.9) in the LMM.

Exercise 7.2 Verify formula (7.3).

It follows that

$$\mathbf{Lia}_i(0) = \tau_i B(0, T_i) \left(F_i(0) + \tau_i \mathbb{E}_{P_{T_i}} \left(L(T_{i-1}, T_i)^2 \right) \right)$$

$$= \tau_i B(0, T_i) F_i(0) \left(1 + \tau_i F_i(0) e^{v_i^2 T_{i-1}} \right)$$

$$= \mathbf{L}_i(0) \left(1 + \tau_i F_i(0) e^{v_i^2 T_{i-1}} \right). \tag{7.4}$$

To value this payment we can set v_i equal to the implied Black volatility $\hat{\sigma}_i^{\text{caplet}}$ of the ith caplet.

7.2 In-arrears swap

The holder of a payer **in-arrears swap** pays a fixed amount $\tau_i K$ in exchange for a floating payment $\tau_i L(T_{i-1}, T_i)$ at time T_{i-1} for $i = 1, \ldots n$, rather than at time T_i as would be the case for a typical interest rate swap. The value at time 0 of an in-arrears payer swap is

$$
\begin{aligned}
\textbf{PSia}(0) &= \sum_{i=1}^{n} \tau_i B(0, T_{i-1}) \mathbb{E}_{P_{T_{i-1}}} (L(T_{i-1}, T_i) - K) \\
&= \sum_{i=1}^{n} \textbf{Lia}_i(0) - K \sum_{i=1}^{n} \tau_i B(0, T_{i-1}).
\end{aligned}
$$

On the other hand, the value of an ordinary payer swap is

$$
\begin{aligned}
\textbf{PS}(0) &= \sum_{i=1}^{n} \tau_i B(0, T_i) \mathbb{E}_{P_{T_i}} (L(T_{i-1}, T_i) - K) \\
&= \sum_{i=1}^{n} \textbf{L}_i(0) - K \sum_{i=1}^{n} \tau_i B(0, T_i).
\end{aligned}
$$

It follows that

$$
\begin{aligned}
\textbf{PSia}(0) = \textbf{PS}(0) &+ \sum_{i=1}^{n} \tau_i^2 B(0, T_i) \mathbb{E}_{P_{T_i}} \left(L(T_{i-1}, T_i)^2 \right) \\
&- K \sum_{i=1}^{n} \tau_i \left(B(0, T_{i-1}) - B(0, T_i) \right).
\end{aligned}
$$

Just like in the case of LIBOR-in-arrears, we can express the convexity correction $\tau_i \mathbb{E}_{P_{T_i}} \left(L(T_{i-1}, T_i)^2 \right)$ in terms of caplet prices or as an analytic expression depending on caplet-implied volatilities.

Portfolio replication

Using (7.2), we can write the in-arrears payer swap price in terms of caplet prices as

$$\mathbf{PSia}(0) = \mathbf{PS}(0) + \sum_{i=1}^{n} 2\tau_i \int_0^{\infty} \mathbf{Cpl}_i(0, K')dK'$$

$$- K \sum_{i=1}^{n} \tau_i \left(B(0, T_{i-1}) - B(0, T_i) \right).$$

Analytic expression in the LMM

Within the LMM, we can apply relationship (7.4) to get the analytic expression

$$\mathbf{PSia}(0) = \mathbf{PS}(0) + \sum_{i=1}^{n} \tau_i^2 B(0, T_i) F_i(0)^2 e^{v_i^2 T_{i-1}}$$

$$- K \sum_{i=1}^{n} \tau_i \left(B(0, T_{i-1}) - B(0, T_i) \right),$$

where v_i is the LMM caplet-implied volatility (5.9).

7.3 Constant-maturity swaps

Take a unit notional amount and a set of dates $t < T_0 < T_1 < \cdots < T_n < \cdots < T_{n+m}$ with accrual periods $\tau_i = T_i - T_{i-1}$. A **constant-maturity swap** (CMS) involves a series of floating payments of an amount $\tau_{i+1} S_{i,i+m}(T_i)$, based on the swap rate setting at time T_i and maturing at T_{i+m}, made in exchange for a fixed amount $\tau_{i+1} K$. For a **set-in-advance** CMS these payments occur at times T_{i+1} for $i = 0, \ldots, n-1$. In the case of a **set-in-arrears** CMS the payment times are T_i for $i = 0, \ldots, n-1$.

Consider a set-in-advance CMS. This is the most common case. The value of the contract at time 0 is

$$\mathbf{CMS}(0) = \sum_{i=0}^{n-1} \tau_{i+1} B(0, T_{i+1}) \mathbb{E}_{P_{T_{i+1}}} \left((S_{i,i+m}(T_i) - K) \right).$$

The ith payment of the CMS occurs at time T_{i+1} and is valued under the forward measure $P_{T_{i+1}}$. Because the swap rate $S_{i,i+m}(t)$ is not a martingale under $P_{T_{i+1}}$, we need to perform a convexity adjustment.

Convexity adjustment for swap rates

Consider a single payment of an amount $S_{i,k}(T_i)$ made at time T_l, where $T_l \geq T_i$ and where

$$S_{i,k}(t) = \frac{B(t, T_i) - B(t, T_k)}{\displaystyle\sum_{j=i+1}^{k} \tau_j B(t, T_j)}$$

is the swap rate setting at time T_i and maturing at T_k. To obtain the value of this payment at time 0 we need to compute the expectation $\mathbb{E}_{P_{T_l}}(S_{i,k}(T_i))$ under the forward measure P_{T_l}.

Since $S_{i,k}(t)$ is not a martingale under P_{T_l}, we perform a change of measure from P_{T_l} to P_A, the forward swap measure associated with taking the swap annuity

$$A_{i,k}(t) = \sum_{j=i+1}^{k} \tau_j B(t, T_j)$$

as numeraire. The swap rate $S_{i,k}(t)$ is a martingale under P_A, so this a more 'natural' choice of measure. The Radon–Nikodym derivative describing this change of measure is

$$\frac{dP_{T_l}}{dP_A} = \frac{A_{i,k}(0)}{B(0, T_l)} \frac{B(T_l, T_l)}{A_{i,k}(T_l)}.$$

It gives

$$\mathbb{E}_{P_{T_l}}(S_{i,k}(T_i)) = \frac{A_{i,k}(0)}{B(0, T_l)} \mathbb{E}_{P_A}\left(S_{i,k}(T_i) \frac{B(T_l, T_l)}{A_{i,k}(T_l)}\right)$$

$$= \frac{A_{i,k}(0)}{B(0, T_l)} \mathbb{E}_{P_A}\left(S_{i,k}(T_i) \frac{B(T_i, T_l)}{A_{i,k}(T_i)}\right).$$

The last equality holds because $\frac{B(t,T_l)}{A_{i,k}(t)}$ is a martingale under P_A.

To evaluate the expectation analytically we need to make some simplifying assumptions. A popular approach, based on the so-called **linear swap-rate model**, is to express the bond $B(T_i, T_l)$ discounted by the annuity $A_{i,k}(T_i)$ as a linear function of the swap rate, namely

$$\frac{B(T_i, T_l)}{A_{i,k}(T_i)} = \alpha + \beta_l S_{i,k}(T_i), \tag{7.5}$$

where α and β_l are deterministic constants. The constant β_l is determined by the fact that $\frac{B(t,T_l)}{A_{i,k}(t)}$ and $S_{i,k}(t)$ are martingales under the forward swap measure P_A, so

$$\frac{B(0, T_l)}{A_{i,k}(0)} = \mathbb{E}_{P_A}\left(\frac{B(T_i, T_l)}{A_{i,k}(T_i)}\right) = \mathbb{E}_{P_A}(\alpha + \beta_l S_{i,k}(T_i)) = \alpha + \beta_l S_{i,k}(0).$$

Therefore

$$\beta_l = \frac{1}{S_{i,k}(0)}\left(\frac{B(0, T_l)}{A_{i,k}(0)} - \alpha\right). \tag{7.6}$$

The parameter α is given by

$$\alpha = \left(\sum_{j=i+1}^{k} \tau_j\right)^{-1} \tag{7.7}$$

as shown in Exercise 7.3. The expectation of the forward swap rate $S_{i,k}(t)$ under the forward measure P_{T_l} is then written as

$$\mathbb{E}_{P_{T_l}}(S_{i,k}(T_i)) = \frac{A_{i,k}(0)}{B(0, T_l)}\mathbb{E}_{P_A}(S_{i,k}(T_i)(\alpha + \beta_l S_{i,k}(T_i)))$$

$$= \frac{A_{i,k}(0)}{B(0, T_l)}\left(\alpha S_{i,k}(0) + \beta_l \mathbb{E}_{P_A}\left(S_{i,k}(T_i)^2\right)\right). \tag{7.8}$$

Exercise 7.3 The parameter α can be determined by using the identity

$$\sum_{j=i+1}^{k} \tau_j \frac{B(T_i, T_j)}{A_{i,k}(T_i)} = 1. \tag{7.9}$$

By substituting (7.5) into the above expression and using (7.6) show that (7.7) holds.

In Section 5.9 we saw that the forward swap rate in the SMM is a drift-less log-normal process, which satisfies the SDE

$$dS_{i,k}(t) = \sigma_{i,k}(t)S_{i,k}(t)dW^A(t),$$

where $\sigma_{i,k}(t)$ is deterministic and $W^A(t)$ is a Brownian motion under the forward swap measure P_A associated with choosing $A_{i,k}(t)$ as numeraire. Solving this SDE, we get

$$S_{i,k}(T_i) = S_{i,k}(0)\exp\left(\int_0^{T_i} \sigma_{i,k}(s)dW^A(s) - \frac{1}{2}\int_0^{T_i} \sigma_{i,k}(s)^2 ds\right).$$

It follows that

$$\mathbb{E}_{P_A}\left(S_{i,k}(T_i)^2\right) = S_{i,k}(0)^2 e^{v_{i,k}^2 T_i}, \qquad (7.10)$$

where

$$v_{i,k} = \sqrt{\frac{1}{T_i}\int_0^{T_i}\sigma_{i,k}(s)^2 ds}$$

is the swaption-implied volatility in the SMM; see (5.34).

Within the SMM the expression (7.8) obtained in the linear swap model becomes an approximation as the two models do not hold simultaneously. Inserting (7.10) into (7.8), we therefore get an approximation

$$\mathbb{E}_{P_{T_l}}(S_{i,k}(T_i)) \approx \frac{A_{i,k}(0)}{B(0,T_l)}\left(\alpha S_{i,k}(0) + \beta_l S_{i,k}(0)^2 e^{v_{i,k}^2 T_i}\right). \qquad (7.11)$$

The accuracy of this expression can be evaluated by estimating the expectation $\mathbb{E}_{P_{T_l}}(S_{i,k}(T_i))$ via the Monte Carlo method.

Returning to the case of the set-in-advance CMS (i.e. $l = i + 1$), we can use the above result to approximate the value of the CMS swap as

$$\mathbf{CMS}(0) \approx \sum_{i=0}^{n-1}\tau_{i+1}A_{i,i+m}(0)\left(\alpha S_{i,i+m}(0) + \beta_{i+1}S_{i,i+m}^2(0)e^{v_{i,i+m}^2 T_i}\right)$$

$$- K\sum_{i=0}^{n-1}\tau_{i+1}B(0,T_{i+1}), \qquad (7.12)$$

where

$$\alpha = \left(\sum_{j=i+1}^{i+m}\tau_j\right)^{-1}, \quad \beta_{i+1} = \frac{1}{S_{i,i+m}(0)}\left(\frac{B(0,T_{i+1})}{A_{i,i+m}(0)} - \alpha\right).$$

We can value the CMS swap at time 0 by setting $v_{i,i+m}$ equal to the implied Black swaption volatility $\hat{\sigma}_{i,i+m}^{\mathrm{swpt}}$ given by the market.

Exercise 7.4   Derive an approximation similar to (7.12) for the price at time 0 of a set-in-arrears CMS.

CMS caps, floors and spread options

A **CMS cap** (or **floor**) is an agreement where the holder receives cash payments on some predefined dates depending on whether a spot swap rate is greater than (less than) some agreed strike rate. Much like a vanilla cap, a CMS cap is a series of caplets. Consider a CMS caplet with unit notional paying at time T_{i+1} on an m-period swap rate setting at time T_i (in this case the swap rate is said to be set in advance). The payoff at time T_{i+1} is

$$\tau_{i+1}(S_{i,i+m}(T_i) - K)^+,$$

where K is the strike rate. A CSM floorlet is defined analogously.

A **CMS spread option** is a derivative instrument whose payoff depends on the difference between two swap rates. Such instruments are traded by investors who have a view on whether the yield curve will steepen or flatten. A typical example would be a CMS cap that pays a coupon at the end of each accrual period if the difference between the 10-year and the two-year swap rates (both swaps rates are normally set at the start of the accrual period) is greater than some predefined strike.

7.4 Ratchet floater

For many instruments an accurate analytic approximation may not be available. In such cases we need to employ a numerical method. Consider an instrument such as a **ratchet floater** or **sticky floater**, which can be thought of as a long position in a floating-rate note based on some reference rate such as LIBOR, along with a short position in a path-dependent cap.

Take a unit notional amount and a set of dates, $0 \le T_0 < T_1 < \cdots < T_n$ with accrual periods $\tau_i = T_i - T_{i-1}$ for $i = 1, \ldots, n$. At time T_i the holder of a ratchet floater receives a coupon payment $\tau_i(F_i(T_{i-1}) + X)$ based on the spot LIBOR rate $F_i(T_{i-1}) = L(T_{i-1}, T_i)$, where X is a preassigned constant spread, in exchange for a coupon payment, which we denote by c_i. The first coupon c_1 is given by the spot LIBOR rate $F_1(T_0)$ plus some spread Y,

$$c_1 = \tau_1(F_1(T_0) + Y).$$

The coupons c_i for $i > 1$ are again given by the spot LIBOR rate plus some spread Y, but subject to the condition that c_i cannot be less than the previous coupon c_{i-1} or greater than c_{i-1} plus some fixed cap $\alpha > 0$. Thus the coupon payments c_i for $i = 2, \ldots, n$ are

$$c_i = c_{i-1} + \min\left((\tau_i(F_i(T_{i-1}) + Y) - c_{i-1})^+, \alpha\right). \tag{7.13}$$

One way of pricing this instrument is to use the LMM. Since the LMM dynamics does not give rise to a known distribution, we need to use Monte

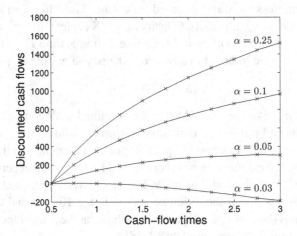

Figure 7.1 Time-0 values of the ratchet floater cash-flow payments at times $T_2, \ldots, T_n$ for various values of the cap α.

Carlo simulation of the forward rates $F_1(t), F_2(t), \ldots, F_n(t)$ under the terminal measure P_{T_n} associated with the T_n-bond as numeraire, as described in Section 6.2. The forward rates are driven by the SDE (6.4) with drift (6.5). The value of the ratchet floater at time 0 is calculated as the Monte Carlo estimate of the expected discounted payoff

$$B(0, T_n) \sum_{i=1}^{n} \mathbb{E}_{P_{T_n}} \left(\frac{\tau_i (F_i(T_{i-1}) + X) - c_i}{B(T_i, T_n)} \right)$$

under the terminal measure P_{T_n}.

Example 7.1
We can apply the calibrated one-factor LMM in Section 6.4 to compute a Monte Carlo estimate of the time 0 value of the cash flow generated by the ratchet floater. As in Example 6.6, we consider a set of dates $0 = T_0 < T_1 < \cdots < T_n$ with accrual periods $\tau_i = 0.25$ for $i = 1, \ldots, n$ and $n = 12$, and with the time T_0 forward LIBOR rates and implied Black caplet volatilities given in Table 6.1. The ratchet floater generates a cash flow consisting of path-dependent payments

$$\tau_i (F_i(T_{i-1}) + X) - c_i$$

occurring at times T_i for $i = 2, \ldots, n$, where c_i is the path-dependent coupon (7.13). The payment at time T_i depends not only on the set of LI-BOR rates at that time but also on previous fixings.

Assuming a 1 million USD notional and taking the constant spreads X and Y to be 0.25%, in Figure 7.1 we plot the time-0 values of the cash-flow payments at $T_2, \ldots, T_n$ for various values of the cap α. For each α the sum of the values along the corresponding line gives the time 0 value of the ratchet floater.

Note that for high values of α we can see a 'snowball' effect, where a high coupon payment leads to even higher payments later. For this reason, the path dependence in the ratchet floater is often referred to as a **snowball** feature. Products of this type are difficult to risk-manage, and have become considerably less popular since the credit crisis.

7.5 Range accruals

A **range accrual swap** is an interest rate swap where the coupon payments on one leg depend on the number of days on which a reference rate (typically a spot LIBOR rate) is within a given range during the accrual period. For instance, consider an investor who receives three-month spot LIBOR (fixed at the start of each accrual period) plus 125 basis points multiplied by the proportion of days on which the spot LIBOR rate stays between 1.0% and 3.0% during the accrual period. If the spot LIBOR rate stays within that range throughout the accrual period, the investor will obtain a return in excess of the three-month spot LIBOR. However, no interest will be accrued for any day on which the reference rate lies outside the range.

Take a unit notional amount and a set of dates $0 \leq T_0 < T_1 < \cdots < T_n$ with accrual periods $\tau_i = T_i - T_{i-1}$ for $i = 1, \ldots, n$. At time T_i for $i = 1, \ldots, n$ the holder of the range accrual swap makes a coupon payment $\tau_i(\alpha F_i(T_{i-1}) + X)$ based on the spot LIBOR rate $F_i(T_{i-1}) = L(T_{i-1}, T_i)$, where α and X are positive constants, in exchange for a payment, called an **accrual coupon**, which depends on the number of days on which a reference rate is within a given range. We denote the days within the accrual period $[T_{i-1}, T_i)$ by $s_i^1, \ldots, s_i^{n_i}$. Here $T_{i-1} \leq s_i^1 < \cdots < s_i^{n_i} < T_i$, where n_i is the total number of days in the period. At time T_i the accrual coupon is

$$c_i = \tau_i \left(\beta F_i(T_{i-1}) + Y \right) \left(\frac{1}{n_i} \sum_{j=1}^{n_i} \mathbf{1}_{\{l \leq F(s_i^j; s_i^j, s_i^j + \delta) \leq u\}} \right), \qquad (7.14)$$

where β are Y positive constants, l is the lower bound, u is the upper bound and $F(s_i^j; s_i^j, s_i^j + \delta) = L(s_i^j, s_i^j + \delta)$ is the spot LIBOR rate at time s_i^j with accrual period δ. To keep the discussion simple we assume δ to be a fixed constant for each $j = 1, \ldots, n_j$.

The value at time 0 of the range accrual swap can be expressed as

$$B(0, T_n) \sum_{i=1}^{n} \mathbb{E}_{P_{T_n}} \left(\frac{c_i - \tau_i(\alpha F_i(T_{i-1}) + X)}{B(T_i, T_n)} \right),$$

where the T_n-bond is taken as numeraire and the expectation is computed under the terminal measure P_{T_n}. We can simulate the evolution through time of the set of forward rates $F_1(t), F_2(t), \ldots, F_n(t)$ under this choice of measure as described in Section 6.2 to obtain a Monte Carlo estimate of the time-0 value. However, the accrual periods of the underlying forward rates in the accrual coupon c_i do not belong to the standard set of reference dates in the LMM. To resolve this problem we can interpolate the rates in the accrual coupon by using the LMM family of forward rates.

In the example above, the accrual coupon is given as a floating rate multiplied by the proportion of days on which the reference rate is in a given range. This is sometimes referred to as a **floating-rate range accrual swap**. Another example is a **fixed-rate range accrual swap**, where the accrual coupon is given by a fixed rate multiplied by the proportion of days on which the reference rate is in a given range. We can value the fixed-rate range accrual by using portfolio replication.

Portfolio replication

We can replicate the fixed-rate range accrual in terms of caplets and floorlets. To see how this might be possible note that the indicator function in (7.14) can be written as

$$\mathbf{1}_{\{u \geq F(s_i^j; s_i^j, s_i^j + \delta)\}} - \mathbf{1}_{\{l > F(s_i^j; s_i^j, s_i^j + \delta)\}}. \tag{7.15}$$

Therefore the accrual coupon c_i can decomposed into a sum of digital floorlets. Digital floorlets can in turn be replicated to an arbitrary degree of accuracy by a bull spread of vanilla floorlets. For example, consider a digital floorlet struck at K with expiry at time t. The digital floorlet pays one unit of currency at time $t + \delta$ if the spot LIBOR $F(t; t, t + \delta)$ is less than or equal to the strike K at time t. The digital floorlet struck at K can be replicated to a desired accuracy controlled by a parameter $\epsilon > 0$ by going long $\frac{1}{\epsilon\delta}$ floorlets struck at $K + \frac{\epsilon}{2}$ and short $\frac{1}{\epsilon\delta}$ floorlets struck at $K - \frac{\epsilon}{2}$. The digital

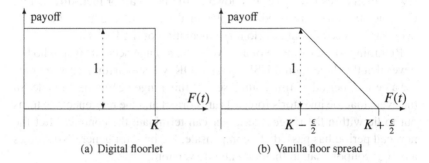

Figure 7.2 The spread payoff closely approximates the digital payoff for small ϵ.

and spread payoffs are compared in Figure 7.2. The portfolio of floorlets has the payoff

$$\frac{1}{\epsilon\delta}\left(\delta\left(K + \frac{\epsilon}{2} - F(t;t,t+\delta)\right)^+ - \delta\left(K - \frac{\epsilon}{2} - F(t;t,t+\delta)\right)^+\right)$$

$$= \begin{cases} 1 & \text{if } F(t;t,t+\delta) < K - \frac{\epsilon}{2}, \\ \frac{1}{\epsilon}(K + \frac{\epsilon}{2} - F(t;t,t+\delta)) & \text{if } K - \frac{\epsilon}{2} \leq F(t;t,t+\delta) < K + \frac{\epsilon}{2}, \\ 0 & \text{otherwise.} \end{cases}$$

In the limit as $\epsilon \to 0$ we recover the digital caplet payoff. Generally, digital floorlets are replicated as bull spreads of vanilla floorlets, where ϵ is either five or 10 basis-points.

Remark 7.2

Floorlets (and caplets) are often referred to as skew dependent instruments. What this means is that the range accrual is highly dependent on the slope of the volatility smile. The volatility smile is the graph of the implied volatility for a given expiry plotted as a function of the strike price. We will discuss the volatility smile in Chapter 8.

Callability: options on an exotic swap

The exotic swaps we discussed in this chapter, such as CMS spread options, range accruals and ratchet floaters, are sometimes **callable**. This means the issuer (i.e. the counterparty who pays the structured coupon) has the right but not the obligation to terminate the exotic swap on a number of the swap fixing dates. Typically, the instrument becomes callable only after a few coupon dates have passed, known as the **non-call** or **lock-out** period. Callable structures are good examples of the type of product where it is necessary to use a Monte Carlo implementation of the LMM.

Returning to the example of an investor in a range accrual swap who believes that the three-month USD spot LIBOR will stay within a given range for a certain period of time, suppose that this range accrual is callable. In the event that the investor's forecasts are correct and the reference rate turns out to lie within the range, the issuer can terminate the contract after the non-call period has passed. To compensate, the investor generally receives a higher coupon than in the non-callable version.

7.6 Trigger swap

A **trigger swap** is a path-dependent option whose payoff depends on whether the path taken by some underlying reference rate reaches a predefined level or barrier. Assume the reference rate to be the spot LIBOR rate and consider the case of an up-and-out trigger swap with trigger level u. If the spot LIBOR rate hits or 'triggers' level u at any point during the life of the swap, then the swap payments cease.

Just like for a range accrual swap, we denote the business days within the accrual period $[T_{i-1}, T_i)$ by $s_i^1, \ldots, s_i^{n_i}$. Assuming the trigger level u has not been hit in any of the previous accrual periods, the swap is still 'alive' at time T_{i-1}. If the spot LIBOR rate $F(s_i^j; s_i^j, s_i^j + \delta)$ is less than u at all times s_i^j for $j = 1, \ldots, n_i$, then the holder agrees to pay a fixed amount $\tau_i K$, where K is some fixed rate, in exchange for a coupon payment $\tau_i(\alpha F_i(T_{i-1}) + X)$, where $\alpha > 0$ is a constant and X is a preassigned constant spread.

Exercise 7.5 Write down the cash flow for the up-and-out trigger swap. Also write down an expression for the value of the swap at time 0 by using the discrete money market account $L(t)$ as numeraire.

8

Volatility smile

In the classical Black–Scholes model volatility is constant. However, in reality options with different strikes need different volatilities to match their market prices. This leads to the notion of implied volatility, which is the unique volatility that must be inserted into the Black–Scholes formula to produce the correct market price. For interest rate derivatives the range of implied volatilities is typically referred to as the volatility smile or skew. The reason for the terms 'smile' or 'skew' is that the graph of the implied volatility as a function of the strike price is typically smile shaped or downward sloping.

In order to accurately value and manage the risk of a portfolio of options, a model should be capable of reproducing the volatility smile observed in the market. In reality this is difficult to achieve. In this chapter we discuss an extension of the Black–Scholes approach referred to as local volatility models (LVM), where volatility is a function of time and the underlying price or rate. A special type of LVM known as the constant elasticity of variance (CEV) model is an extension of the LMM capable of capturing the skew. Examples of tractable local volatility models such as the normal model, CEV and displaced-diffusion models will be analysed.

Local volatility models are an improvement on Black's approach, but are unable to reproduce smile-shaped curves. Stochastic volatility models were introduced to overcome this limitation. In these models the volatility of the underlying price or rate is itself a stochastic process driven by its own Brownian motion. The stochastic volatility model touched upon in this chapter is known as SABR. It is a model of a single forward interest rate (either the forward LIBOR rate or the forward swap rate), which has become one of the standard approaches when it comes to modelling the volatility smile.

8.1   Black's formula revisited

Black's formula is the standard market formula for caplets. The key assumption is that the forward LIBOR rate $F_i(t)$ is a driftless log-normal process under the forward measure P_{T_i}, which makes it possible to derive Black's caplet formula (2.24) with volatility (5.9).

In practice the caplet price is quoted in terms of the implied volatility $\hat{\sigma}_i^{\text{caplet}}$. The actual caplet price is recovered by substituting the implied volatility into Black's formula (2.24). Taking the actual caplet prices given by the market for different values of the strike K and then solving for the implied volatility, one can see that $\hat{\sigma}_i^{\text{caplet}}$ depends on K. Furthermore, the graph of $\hat{\sigma}_i^{\text{caplet}}$ versus K will shift to the left or right when the forward rate changes. Therefore the implied volatility is also a function of the current forward rate $F_i(t)$. This indicates that, in fact, the forward LIBOR rate $F_i(t)$ is not a log-normal process.

We can further verify this by using a set of market caplet prices to estimate the distribution of the forward rate. The price at time t of the ith caplet is

$$\mathbf{Cpl}_i(0; K) = \tau_i B(0, T_i) \mathbb{E}_{P_{T_i}} ((F_i(T_{i-1}) - K)^+)$$

$$= \tau_i B(0, T_i) \int_K^\infty (x - K) \phi_{F_i(T_{i-1})}(x) dx,$$

where we have made the dependence of the caplet price on K explicit, and where $\phi_{F_i(T_{i-1})}(x)$ is the probability density of $F_i(T_{i-1})$ under the forward measure P_{T_i}. Differentiating twice with respect to the strike price K, we have

$$\frac{\partial^2 \mathbf{Cpl}_i(0; K)}{\partial K^2} = \tau_i B(0, T_i) \phi_{F_i(T_{i-1})}(K). \tag{8.1}$$

Given caplet prices for a range of strikes, we can estimate this partial derivative and plot the probability density of $F_i(T_{i-1})$. For typical market data this will not be log-normal.

The relationship between the volatility in Black's formula and the actual volatility of the underlying forward-rate process is much more complicated than that given by (5.9). For this reason, the implied volatility has been described as 'the wrong number put in the wrong formula to get the right price'.

Risk management and hedging

The volatility smile has important consequences for risk management. Consider a caplet with strike K written on a forward rate $F_i(t)$ and expiring at time T_{i-1}. We write Black's formula (2.25) as

$$\mathbf{Cpl}_i^{\text{mkt}}(t; K, F_i(t)) = \mathbf{Cpl}_i^{\text{Black}}(t; \hat{\sigma}_i(K, F_i(t)), K, F_i(t)),$$

where the dependence on the strike K and the forward rate $F_i(t)$ is made explicit. The delta of the caplet is given by differentiating with respect to the forward price,

$$\frac{\partial \mathbf{Cpl}_i^{\text{mkt}}}{\partial F_i} = \frac{\partial \mathbf{Cpl}_i^{\text{Black}}}{\partial F_i} + \frac{\partial \mathbf{Cpl}_i^{\text{Black}}}{\partial \hat{\sigma}_i} \frac{\partial \hat{\sigma}_i}{\partial F_i}. \tag{8.2}$$

The first term on the right-hand side can be shown to be equal to $N(d_+)$, where

$$d_+ = \frac{\ln \frac{F_i(t)}{K} + \frac{1}{2}\hat{\sigma}_i(K, F_i(t))^2(T_{i-1} - t)}{\hat{\sigma}_i(K, F_i(t)) \sqrt{T_{i-1} - t}}.$$

The second term is the vega computed from Black's formula, multiplied by the rate of change of implied volatility due to a change in the underlying forward rate. It can be thought of as a correction term that we need to apply to the delta given by Black's formula to give the correct delta hedge. To calculate this term we need to know the functional dependence of the implied volatility on $F_i(t)$. To this end we need a new model for the forward-rate process that can accurately price all caplets for each strike K and exercise date T. Specifically, the graph of Black's implied volatility given by the model price must closely match that given in the market.

A popular approach to this problem is the CEV model. As we shall see, it can be approximated by a shifted log-normal process. This gives an analytic formula, which we can use to price each caplet. Given a model formula, we can infer the implied volatility in Black's formula and therefore estimate the rate of change in the implied volatility due to a change in the forward rate.

Typically, the CEV model parameters are calibrated to today's smile, enabling the model to correctly reproduce the market prices. However, local volatility models like CEV fail to capture the dynamics of the smile correctly. Though the model is consistent with the market, the delta hedge calculated by the model may be incorrect and in fact worse than that computed from Black's formula.

8.2 Normal model

In Section 5.2 we derived Black's caplet formula by assuming that the forward rate $F_i(t)$ follows a log-normal process. Here we obtain a pricing formula for caplets based on the assumption that the dynamics of the forward rate can be modelled by a normal process. Namely, for any $i = 1, \ldots, n$ the forward rate $F_i(t)$ is assumed to evolve as

$$dF_i(t) = \sigma_i(t)dW^{T_i}(t), \tag{8.3}$$

where $\sigma_i(t)$ is a deterministic time-dependent volatility and $W^{T_i}(t)$ is a Brownian motion under the forward measure P_{T_i}. This gives

$$F_i(T_{i-1}) = F_i(t) + \int_t^{T_{i-1}} \sigma_i(s)dW^{T_i}(s)$$

for any $t \le T_{i-1}$. The difference $F_i(T_{i-1}) - F_i(t)$ is independent of $\mathcal{F}_t$ and normally distributed with mean 0 and variance

$$s_i^2 = \int_t^{T_{i-1}} \sigma_i^2(s)ds.$$

When it comes to modelling the forward-rate dynamics, many practitioners argue that the normal model provides a better fit to market data than the log-normal model. However, as the forward rate is normally distributed, it can become negative in finite time with non-zero probability.

Caplet price

Recall that the holder of an interest rate caplet receives $\tau_i(L(T_{i-1}, T_i) - K)^+$ at time T_i, where K is the strike rate. Without loss of generality, we can assume a unit notional. Then the price at time t of the caplet is

$$\mathbf{Cpl}_i(t) = \tau_i B(t, T_i) \mathbb{E}_{P_{T_i}}((F_i(T_{i-1}) - K)^+|\mathcal{F}_t)$$

$$= \tau_i B(t, T_i) \left(\mathbb{E}_{P_{T_i}}\left(F_i(T_{i-1})\mathbf{1}_{\{F_i(T_{i-1}) \ge K\}}\middle| \mathcal{F}_t \right) - K\mathbb{E}_{P_{T_i}}\left(\mathbf{1}_{\{F_i(T_{i-1}) \ge K\}}\middle| \mathcal{F}_t \right) \right). \tag{8.4}$$

The second expectation can be evaluated as

$$\mathbb{E}_{P_{T_i}}\left(\mathbf{1}_{\{F_i(T_{i-1}) \geq K\}}\middle|\mathcal{F}_t\right) = P_{T_i}\{(F_i(T_{i-1}) \geq K)|\mathcal{F}_t\}$$

$$= P_{T_i}\left\{\frac{F_i(T_{i-1}) - F_i(t)}{s_i} \geq \frac{K - F_i(t)}{s_i}\right\}$$

$$= N\left(\frac{F_i(t) - K}{s_i}\right) = N(d_1),$$

where $N(\cdot)$ denotes the cumulative normal distribution and

$$d_1 = \frac{F_i(t) - K}{\sqrt{\int_t^{T_{i-1}} \sigma_i^2(s)ds}}.$$

Next we evaluate the first expectation in (8.4):

$$\mathbb{E}_{T_i}\left(F_i(T_{i-1})\mathbf{1}_{\{F_i(T_{i-1}) \geq K\}}\middle|\mathcal{F}_t\right) = \int_K^{\infty} \frac{x}{\sqrt{2\pi}s_i}e^{-\frac{1}{2}\left(\frac{x-F_i(t)}{s_i}\right)^2}dx$$

$$= \frac{1}{\sqrt{2\pi}}\int_{\frac{K-F_i(t)}{s_i}}^{\infty}(F_i(t) + s_i z)e^{-\frac{1}{2}z^2}dz$$

$$= F_i(t)N(d_1) + \frac{s_i}{\sqrt{2\pi}}e^{-\frac{1}{2}d_1^2}.$$

Therefore, the value at time t of the caplet is

$$\mathbf{Cpl}_i^{\text{Normal}}(t) = \tau_i B(t, T_i)\left((F_i(t) - K)N(d_1) + \frac{s_i}{\sqrt{2\pi}}e^{-\frac{1}{2}d_1^2}\right).$$

We use the superscript ^{Normal} to highlight the fact that the formula for the caplet price has been derived under the assumption that the forward rate follows a normal process (8.3) as opposed to the more typical assumption of a log-normal process.

The volatility skew produced by the normal process is shown in Figure 8.5.

8.3 CEV process

The **constant elasticity of variance** (CEV) model is an alternative to the Black–Scholes framework and was originally developed to describe a stock price process. It can be used to capture the volatility smile.

In the CEV model of the forward rate we assume that $F_i(t)$ evolves according to

$$dF_i(t) = \sigma_i(t)F_i(t)^\beta dW^{T_i}(t), \qquad (8.5)$$

where $0 \le \beta \le 1$, $\sigma_i(t)$ is a deterministic time-dependent volatility and $W^{T_i}(t)$ is a Brownian motion under the forward measure P_{T_i}.

The CEV process as written above applies only up to the stopping time

$$\tau = \inf\{t > 0 : F_i(t) = 0\},$$

or otherwise $F_i(t)^\beta$ might be imaginary if $F_i(t)$ became negative. To overcome this restriction we need to apply some boundary condition. For simplicity we assume the boundary condition $F_i(t) = 0$ for all $t \ge \tau$. In other words, once the forward rate becomes zero, it remains at zero for all time. For this choice of boundary condition the SDE (8.5) has solutions for all β.

From (8.5) we can see that the forward rate is log-normal if $\beta = 1$, while it is a normal process for $\beta = 0$. By carefully choosing β, we can fit the forward-rate dynamics to market data more accurately than using either the normal or log-normal model.

Choosing β

Market practice is to put $\beta = 0.5$. However, for $\beta = 0.5$ the origin becomes an absorbing barrier. For a given time t, all paths that reach zero before t become 'absorbed', so the probability density function becomes the sum of a sharp delta distribution at the origin, plus a non-central chi-squared distribution for values of the forward rate greater than zero. Moreover, in the limit as $t \to \infty$ all paths eventually reach zero, and the probability density converges to the delta function.

When the rates are relatively high, the proportion of paths that reach zero is typically low. This is shown in Figure 8.1, where 10 000 paths of the CEV process (8.5) are simulated starting from $F_i(0) = 5\%$ with $\beta = 0.5$ and $\sigma_i = 0.1$, and the values of the forward rate $F_i(t)$ at time $t = 1$ are then used to form a histogram. However, when rates are low, for example $F_i(0) = 1\%$, the proportion of paths that reach zero can be high, over 10% in Figure 8.2. In a low-interest-rate environment this feature of the model can have a significant impact on valuation and risk management.

When the initial value of the forward rate is low, choosing a different boundary condition such that a return to $F_i(t) > 0$ is possible after the stopping time τ has been reached is one way of overcoming the problem in Figure 8.2. The most popular approach, however, is to simplify the CEV

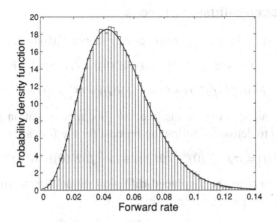

Figure 8.1 Simulated distribution of the forward rate $F_i(t)$ at time $t = 1$ for the CEV process when the initial value is $F_i(0) = 5\%$, with $\beta = 0.5$ and $\sigma_i = 0.1$.

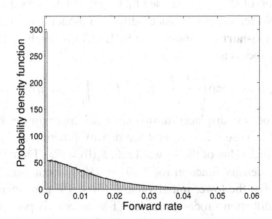

Figure 8.2 Simulated distribution of the forward rate $F_i(t)$ at time $t = 1$ for the CEV process when the initial value is $F_i(0) = 1\%$, with $\beta = 0.5$ and $\sigma_i = 0.1$.

process by transforming it to what is known as the displaced-diffusion process or shifted log-normal process.

8.4 Displaced-diffusion process

We first perform a Taylor expansion of $F_i(t)$ about $F_i(0)$ to get

$$F_i(t)^\beta = F_i(0)^\beta + \beta F_i(0)^{\beta-1}(F_i(t) - F_i(0)) + O\big((F_i(t) - F_i(0))^2\big)$$
$$= F_i(0)^{\beta-1}\big(\beta F_i(t) + (1-\beta)F_i(0)\big) + O\big((F_i(t) - F_i(0))^2\big).$$

Omitting the higher-order terms, we use this approximation in place of $F_i(t)^\beta$ in (8.5) to define the following process for the forward rate:

$$dF_i(t) = \sigma_i(t)F_i(0)^{\beta-1}\big(\beta F_i(t) + (1-\beta)F_i(0)\big)\,dW^{T_i}(t). \qquad (8.6)$$

This is referred to as the **displaced-diffusion model** for the forward rate. The above can be more conveniently written as

$$d(F_i(t) + \alpha) = \sigma_i^{D}(t)\,(F_i(t) + \alpha)\,dW^{T_i}(t), \qquad (8.7)$$

where

$$\alpha = \frac{(1-\beta)F_i(0)}{\beta}, \qquad \sigma_i^{D}(t) = \beta F_i(0)^{\beta-1}\sigma_i(t). \qquad (8.8)$$

We call α the **displaced-diffusion coefficient**.

By inspection of (8.7), we can see that $F_i(t) + \alpha$ follows a log-normal process. For this reason the displaced-diffusion model is often referred to as the **shifted log-normal model**. The SDE (8.7) is much more tractable than the CEV process and can be solved to give

$$F_i(t) = (F_i(0) + \alpha)\exp\left(-\frac{1}{2}\int_0^t \sigma_i^{D}(s)^2 ds + \int_0^t \sigma_i^{D}(s)dW^{T_i}(s)\right) - \alpha.$$

How well does the displaced-diffusion model approximate the original CEV process? In Figure 8.3 we plot the density function of $F_i(t)$ at time $t = 1$ for an initial value of the forward rate $F_i(0) = 5\%$. Figure 8.4 shows the probability density function for $F_i(0) = 1\%$. In both figures $\beta = 0.5$ and $\sigma_i = 0.1$. For the lower initial value $F_i(0) = 1\%$ agreement between the displaced-diffusion process and the CEV process is poor. Moreover, in the case of the displaced-diffusion model the forward rate can become negative, while the CEV process suffers from the problems outlined in Section 8.3. However, for the initial value $F_i(0) = 5\%$ agreement is very good.

Caplet pricing formula

A main advantage of the displaced-diffusion model is that $F_i(T_{i-1}) + \alpha$ is log-normally distributed, so we can use Black's caplet formula derived in

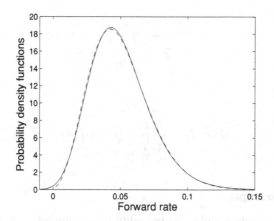

Figure 8.3 The probability density of $F_i(t)$ at $t = 1$ for the displaced-diffusion process (solid line) and the CEV process (dashed line) when $F_i(0) = 5\%$, with $\beta = 0.5$ and $\sigma_i = 0.1$.

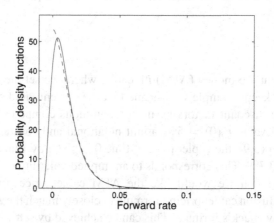

Figure 8.4 The probability density of $F_i(t)$ at $t = 1$ for the displaced-diffusion process (solid line) and the CEV process (dashed line) when $F_i(0) = 1\%$, with $\beta = 0.5$ and $\sigma_i = 0.1$.

Section 5.2. Note that for the ith caplet the price at time t can be written as

$$\mathbf{Cpl}_i(t) = \tau_i B(t, T_i) \mathbb{E}_{P_{T_i}} \left(((F_i(T_{i-1}) + \alpha) - (K + \alpha))^+ \big| \mathcal{F}_t \right).$$

The price of the caplet is then given by

$$\mathbf{Cpl}_i(t) = \tau_i B(t, T_i) \left((F_i(t) + \alpha) N(d_+) - (K + \alpha) N(d_-) \right),$$

where

$$d_+ = \frac{\ln \frac{F_i(t)+\alpha}{K+\alpha} + \frac{1}{2} \int_t^{T_{i-1}} \left(\sigma_i^D(s)\right)^2 ds}{\sqrt{\int_t^{T_{i-1}} \left(\sigma_i^D(s)\right)^2 ds}},$$

and

$$d_- = d_+ - \sqrt{\int_t^{T_{i-1}} \left(\sigma_i^D(s)\right)^2 ds}.$$

Numerical example

In the next example we plot the volatility skew implied by the displaced-diffusion caplet pricing formula for a number of different values of the displaced-diffusion coefficient α. Recall that the volatility skew or smile is the implied volatility (given as a function of the strike K) that must be inserted into Black's formula (2.24) to reproduce the price given by the model.

Example 8.1
Consider the at-the-money (ATM) ith caplet where we set the expiry date $T_{i-1} = 1$. To keep it simple we assume that the current yield curve is flat and calculate discount factors by using continuous compounding at 5%. For an initial value $F_i(0) = 5\%$, a unit notational and constant volatility $\sigma_i(t) = 0.2$ in (5.9), the caplet price at time 0 is given by Black's formula (5.8) as 0.003 789. This corresponds to an implied volatility of 20%.

For comparison we would like the ATM caplet price given by the displaced-diffusion caplet pricing formula to closely match the ATM caplet price given by Black's formula. This can be achieved by setting

$$\sigma_i^D(t) = \frac{\sigma_i(t)F_i(t)}{F_i(t) + \alpha}. \tag{8.9}$$

For example, if $\alpha = 0.05$, then $\sigma^D(t) = 0.1$, producing a caplet price of 0.003 793, very close to that given by Black's formula.

In Figure 8.5 we plot the volatility for various values of the displacement coefficient α. We can see that the displaced-diffusion model produces a monotonically decreasing curve.

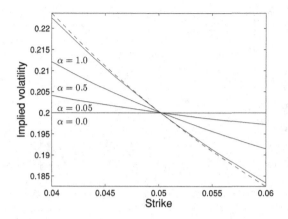

Figure 8.5 Volatility skew produced by the displaced-diffusion model for different values of α. For comparison the volatility skew for the normal model is also shown (dashed line).

Remark 8.2

A problem with the CEV model is that it fails to describe the skew/smile dynamics correctly. For an increase in the forward rate the implied volatility curve moves to the left, while if the forward rate decreases, the curve moves to the right. This behaviour does not match empirical observations.

   We can explore the dynamics by increasing the initial forward rate and recalculating the implied volatility. For instance, consider the volatility skew implied by the displaced-diffusion caplet pricing formula. Taking the ATM caplet described in Example 8.1 for the case when $\alpha = 0.05$, in Figure 8.6 we plot the implied volatility for $F_i(0) = 0.05$ (solid line) and then for a higher value of 0.055 (dashed line). The implied-volatility curve moves to the left. This means that the sign of the correction term in (8.2) is incorrect and the model leads to a delta hedge that performs worse than that given by Black's model.

8.5 Stochastic volatility

We conclude with some remarks on the **SABR model**, which was developed to match the volatility smile observed in the market. It is a model of a single forward rate (a forward LIBOR rate or forward swap rate), popular

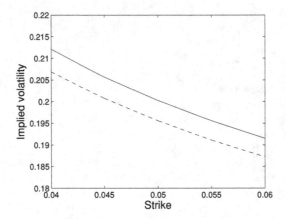

Figure 8.6 Volatility skew produced by the displaced-diffusion model for $\alpha = 0.5$. The forward rate changes from $F_i(0) = 0.05$ (solid line) to 0.055 (dashed line).

among practitioners due to its relative simplicity and analytic tractability. In particular, it yields an accurate closed-form approximation to the implied volatility of a European option on the rate.

Consider the case of a forward LIBOR rate. In the SABR model $F_i(t)$ is assumed to satisfy

$$dF_i(t) = F_i(t)^\beta \sigma_i(t) dW^{T_i}(t),$$
$$d\sigma_i(t) = v\sigma_i(t) dZ^{T_i}(t),$$

where $W^{T_i}(t)$ and $Z^{T_i}(t)$ are Brownian motions under the forward measure P_{T_i} such that

$$dW^{T_i}(t) dZ^{T_i}(t) = \rho dt$$

with constant instantaneous correlation ρ. The process $\sigma_i(t)$ is the stochastic volatility of $F_i(t)$, while v is the constant volatility of $\sigma_i(t)$, referred to by practitioners as the 'vol-of-vol'. The parameter ranges are $v \geq 0, 0 \leq \beta < 1$ and $-1 < \rho < 1$.

The model provides an analytic approximation of the implied volatility σ_i^{caplet} for a caplet in terms of the parameters β, ρ, v and initial conditions

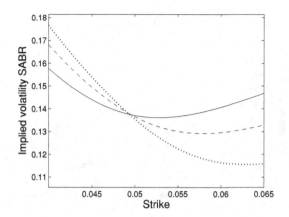

Figure 8.7 Implied volatility given by the SABR formula (8.11) for $F_i(0) = 5\%$, $\sigma_i(0) = 3\%$, $\beta = 0.5$, $\nu = 50\%$ and ρ set equal to 0.0 (solid line), -0.25 (dashed line) and -0.5 (dotted line). Time to expiry T_{i-1} is equal to 1.

$F_i(0)$ and $\sigma_i(0)$. It is given by

$$\sigma_i^{\text{caplet}} = \frac{\sigma_i(0)}{(F_i(0)K)^{(1-\beta)/2}\left(1 + \frac{(1-\beta)^2}{24}\ln^2\frac{f}{K} + \frac{(1-\beta)^4}{1920}\ln^4\frac{F_i(0)}{K} + \ldots\right)}\left(\frac{z}{\chi(z)}\right)$$

$$\left(1 + \left(\frac{(1-\beta)^2}{24}\frac{\sigma_i(0)^2}{(F_i(0)K)^{(1-\beta)}} + \frac{\rho\beta\nu\sigma_i(0)}{4(F_i(0)K)^{(1-\beta)/2}} + \frac{2-3\rho^2}{24}\nu^2\right)T_{i-1} + \cdots\right),$$

$$(8.11)$$

where

$$z = \frac{\nu}{\sigma_i(0)}(F_i(0)K)^{(1-\beta)/2}\ln\frac{F_i(0)}{K}$$

and $\chi(z)$ is defined by

$$\chi(z) = \ln\left(\frac{\sqrt{1-2\rho z + z^2} + z - \rho}{1-\rho}\right).$$

This formula was derived by using singular-perturbation analysis. In the case of the forward swap rate an analogous formula holds true for the swaption-implied volatility. The actual derivation of (8.11) is quite involved and for that reason not presented here. Instead, we briefly discuss the qualitative behaviour of the implied volatility subject to changes in the model parameters and initial conditions.

The principal effect of an increase in the initial volatility $\sigma_i(0)$ is an

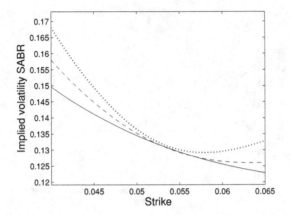

Figure 8.8 Implied volatility given by the SABR formula (8.11) for $F_i(0) =$ 5%, $\sigma_i(0) = 3\%$, $\beta = 0.5$, $\rho = -0.25\%$ and ν set equal to 20% (solid line), 35% (dashed line) and 50% (dotted line). Time to expiry T_{i-1} is equal to 1.

upwards parallel shift in the Black implied-volatility smile, while a change in β from 1 to 0 will cause the slope of the smile to steepen. This closely matches the behaviour of the CEV model (8.5). In the SABR model we can also change the slope of the smile by varying ρ. In fact, when calibrating to market data, the practice is to fix β while letting ρ vary. In Figure 8.7 we can see that the slope of the smile steepens as ρ decreases from 0 to -0.5. We observe an increase in out-of-the-money implied volatility and a decrease in in-the-money implied volatility. The vol-of-vol ν introduces curvature to the smile, helping to fit the model to smile-shaped curves. An increase in ν causes the curvature of the implied volatility curve to increase as shown in Figure 8.8. We observe an increase in both in-the-money and out-of-the-money implied volatility.

One of the key reasons why the model has effectively become the market standard is that it captures the dynamics of the smile correctly. As the forward rate increases, the implied-volatility curve moves to the right, while if the forward rate decreases, the curve moves to the left. This behaviour is shown in Figure 8.9. In this figure we plot the implied volatility (8.11) as a function of strike for two different values of the forward rate $F_i(0)$.

Indeed it is market practice to consider the SABR formula as exact. In the case of a swaption for a given expiry and tenor, a practitioner would calibrate the SABR-model-implied volatilities across the strike dimension

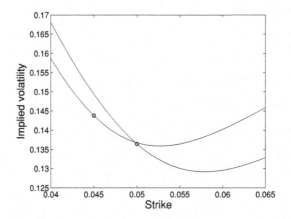

Figure 8.9 SABR-implied volatility for $\beta = 0.5, \sigma_i = 3\%, \rho = -0.25$ and $\nu = 50\%$. The at-the-money implied volatility is depicted by circles. As the forward rate $F_i(0)$ increases (from 4.5% to 5%), the implied volatility curve moves to the right. Time to expiry T_{i-1} is equal to 1.

to the prices quoted in the market. The calibrated formula is then used to give the implied volatility for a given strike.

The SABR model has, nonetheless, a number of shortcomings. It is a model of a single forward rate, unlike the LMM, which describes the joint evolution of a set of forward LIBOR rates under a common measure. It needs to be separately calibrated for each expiry; that is, the model parameters are different for different option expiries. For vanilla options this is not an issue as their value depends solely on the terminal distribution at expiry. However, for exotics the model would need to reproduce the empirically observed term structure of volatility smiles across different expiries.

Index

accrual coupon, 139
affine term structure model, 48

Bermudan swaption, 59
Black's formula, 37, 85, 107
Black–Derman–Toy model, 43
Black–Krasinski model, 43
bond option, 30
bootstrapping, 19

cap, 33
caplet, 33
constant elasticity of variance (CEV)
  model, 147
constant-maturity swap (CMS)
  cap, 136
  floor, 136
convexity adjustment, 130
convexity correction, 130
convexity-corrected forward rate, 130
coupon rate, 10
Cox–Ingersoll–Ross model, 43

day-count conventions, 9
discount bond, 2
discounted value, 4
displaced-diffusion model, 150
Dothan model, 43

Euro Interbank Offered Rate
  (EURIBOR), 3

fixed-coupon bond, 10
flat volatility, 37
floating-coupon bond, 10
floating-rate note, 10
floor, 33
floorlet, 33
forward bond price, 7
forward contract, 27
forward curve, 8
forward discount factor, 7
forward measure, 25
forward rate, 6
  continuously compounded, 7
  convexity-corrected, 130
  instantaneous, 8

forward rate agreement (FRA), 5
forward swap measure, 106

Heath–Jarrow–Morton (HJM) model, 67
  Gaussian, 71
  multi-factor, 78
Hull–White model, 43, 51
Hull–White short-rate model
  bond option formula, 53
  forward measure, 58
  two-factor, 62
hypersphere decomposition, 114

implied Black volatility
  for caplets, 37
  for swaptions, 38
instantaneous forward rate, 8
instantaneous short rate, 8
interest rate swap, 11
  constant-maturity, 133
  forward-starting, 12
  in-arrears, 132
  length of, 12
  payer, 12
  receiver, 12
  reset dates, 12
  settlement dates, 12
  start date, 12
  trigger, 142

Jamshidian's trick, 55

LIBOR market model (LMM), 84
  calibration, 121
  discrete money market account, 90
  instantaneous correlation, 84, 100
  instantaneous volatility, 84
  rank reduction, 113
  terminal measure, 90
LIBOR-in-arrears, 129
London Interbank Offered Rate
  (LIBOR), 1, 3

martingale measure, 23
Mercurio–Moraleda model, 76
Merton model, 43, 44
model

159

Printed in the United States
By Bookmasters